Kill All The Lawyers?

Also by Sloan Bashinsky

Home Buyers: Lambs to the Slaughter?
Selling Your Home, $weet Home

Kill All the Lawyers?

A Client's Guide to Hiring, Firing, Using, and Suing Lawyers

by

SLOAN BASHINSKY

Prentice Hall Press ● New York

I suspect that the disclaimer was invented by some lawyer who loved to give advice but didn't want to be held responsible for having given it. In reading this book, please keep in mind that it was written to assist you in your dealings with a lawyer. It was not written to advise you how to handle other legal matters, except in the situations so indicated. Regardless of how you may feel about lawyers, the legal system is complex and full of hidden dangers for the lay person, not to mention most lawyers. For that reason, you cannot reasonably expect to come out ahead in a legal matter without some assistance from a lawyer.

Published by Prentice Hall Press
A Division of Simon & Schuster, Inc.
PRENTICE HALL PRESS is a trademark of Simon & Schuster, Inc.

Library of Congress number 86-549

ISBN 0-671-60468-6

Manufactured in the United States of America

10 9 8 7 6 5 4 3 2 1

First Edition

To my law professor, SAM BEATTY,
who instilled in me an understanding of the law
and who taught me to think

Acknowledgements

To everyone who helped, especially the following, my thanks:

FRED BONNIE, for encouraging me to write,
BOB SEHLINGER, my first publisher, who gave me the idea,
DEDE SELF and her word processor, for the manuscript,
JANE, my wife, for editing out the legal mumbo jumbo,
my lawyer and lay friends, for their critiques and suggestions, and
WILLIAM SHAKESPEARE, for the title

Let God kill him who himself does not know but
presumes to show others the way.
—G. I. GURDJIEFF,
Meetings With Remarkable Men

With that admonition very much in mind, and with full knowledge
that many other lawyers could probably do this subject more justice, I
offer this book in the hope that it will help people in their dealings
with lawyers and the legal system.

Contents

Opening Remarks

WHEN MY PUBLISHER asked me to write a book about lawyers and lay people, I was both flattered at the suggestion and awed at the responsibility of such an undertaking. I suspect that I was asked because of my tendency to be a "bridge burner," a trait that has left me and some of my professional colleagues with mixed feelings about each other. While it's rewarding to be thought of as being courageous (less flattering adjectives have also been used), it's discouraging to know that the only time some of my lawyer friends wish to be seen with me is in the steam room of the YMCA—where they are not likely to be recognized.

I started writing books with what has politely been called painful honesty only after learning that for the subjects I am qualified to address there is no other effective way to get the message across. Preferring to give no loaf than half a loaf, I agreed to undertake this book on condition that, as with my previous ones, I could write it as I saw it. My publisher agreed to my demand, retaining, however, the power to censure my First Amendment right of free speech. I also vaguely recall something being said about not wanting to be sued for libel. So I wrote the book and, to my surprise, most of it survived the editing process.

As with the yin-yang duality found in Eastern philosophy, the law is a system of give and take, as symbolized by the statue of the blindfolded woman holding the balanced scales of justice. In an attempt to do the right thing—provide justice—the legal system seldom delivers what everyone wants from it. This give and take is, I feel, a major cause of lay misunderstanding of lawyers and the legal system. For instance, every case, like it or not, has two (sometimes three or four) sides to it, and there are good and bad lawyers, judges, juries, cases, and, yes, clients.

The popular misapplication of the famous quotation from Shakespeare's *King Henry VI*, "The first thing we do, let's kill all the lawyers," demonstrates the confusion. Few people—including lawyers—know that Shakespeare probably meant to pay a compliment to

1

lawyers, not to disparage them. The character who made that statement was a scoundrel with revolutionary intent. He knew very well that the government could not be overthrown without eliminating all of the lawyers, for, in those days, it was felt that lawyers were the bastion of law and order, the preservers of personal rights. Today? Well, perhaps killing some might not be such a bad idea, but all of them? Shakespeare would roll over in his grave!

The image of the legal profession certainly needs to be improved. However, the simple truth is that an imperfect society breeds certain professions that are naturally unpopular. Among them, I'm sad to say, is the legal profession—my profession.

The lawyer whose client or cause is unpopular is not going to be well liked, no matter how capably or ethically he performs. "How can you defend a guilty person" is the most common question asked of trial lawyers. For a trial lawyer, the answer is simple: If he judges his client guilty, he violates his role as an advocate and is no longer functioning as a lawyer. When a lawyer abandons his normal role and assumes to judge his client, that places the client and the legal system at risk.

Be that as it may, a good lawyer can be invaluable, even save futures and lives—and not just those of people accused of murder or rape. A bad lawyer, on the other hand, can cause more grief than all of the king's men can undo. But no lawyer, regardless of ability or diligence, can do much for a client who will not follow advice, talks instead of listening, has read two dozen "how to be your own lawyer" books, or is a con-man or know-it-all. In other words, a jerk.

So I do not plan either to kill or to spare all of the lawyers, nor am I going to give you many suggestions about being your own lawyer. This book is mainly about two things: dealing with lawyers and being a client. Lawyers, sometimes unfortunately, are human, meaning that you, the client, must shoulder part of the responsibility for the relationship to work well. And I am going to tell you how to do that.

It is my hope that, after reading this book, you will have a better understanding of lawyers, of how and when to use one, and what to do if one abuses you. And that, ladies and gentlemen, concludes my opening remarks. Now it will be up to you to consider the evidence that will be presented, then decide if I have accomplished what I set out to do.

Part I

LEGAL SNARES

1

The Lottery

MANY PEOPLE HAVE never used a lawyer. Those who have usually did it only one or two times, to have a will or simple business agreement drawn up, to buy a home, or to get a divorce. As a result, few people understand lawyers or how they operate, and most people are afraid of lawyers. All of this makes it very difficult to hire the right lawyer when the need arises. So does what follows.

About 40,000 new lawyers are dumped into the legal system each year. These new lawyers do not have to serve an internship to become licensed to practice their profession. In fact, all that they must do is graduate from a three-year law school program and pass a state bar examination. Then, without any practical experience whatsoever, they can begin "practicing" on you. Just think about it: a twenty-five-year-old legal beagle representing you in a divorce, writing a complicated trust into your will, advising you how to buy a business, or handling a major damage suit for injuries received by your child in a school bus wreck. Any licensed lawyer, regardless of his experience, can handle any of these cases if he wants to—if you let him.

"But," you say to yourself, "I won't use a new lawyer for my case; I will get an older, more experienced lawyer." Perhaps, but Chief Justice of the United States Supreme Court Warren E. Burger still doesn't think that your chances are very good for getting an honest, competent lawyer. For instance, in 1974 he said, "Up to one-third or one-half of the lawyers coming into our courts were not really qualified to render fully adequate representation." Later he was quoted as saying that "75 to 90 percent of American trial lawyers are incompetent, dishonest, or both."

Let's compare lawyers to doctors for a moment. The latter are required to serve an internship after graduating from medical school before they can practice medicine on their own. During their internship, they are supervised by licensed and more skilled and experienced doctors. After completing the internship, they are then allowed to practice "general" medicine—the simple stuff like common colds, headaches, the flu, and common diseases. They are not allowed to work in the areas of specialized medicine such as orthopedics, neurosurgery, psychiatry, ophthalmology, internal medicine, and so forth. Nor can they buy malpractice insurance that would insure them in specialized areas of medicine.

In order to specialize, doctors must spend several more years under the supervision of specialist doctors. Then they are "certified" by the state medical agency to practice medicine in that specialty. Once they receive their specialty designation, they can list their specialty in the Yellow Pages and medical directories and on their stationery and business cards. In other words, it's easy to find a medical specialist, and when you call one for an appointment, you can probably count on his knowing what he is doing.

Because of the lack of supervised certification of legal specialties, many states prohibit lawyers from advertising their specialties. In a way, that is good, because it reduces the chances of an unsuspecting client wandering into the office of a lawyer who has misrepresented his expertise as, say, a criminal or tax lawyer. However, it sure makes it difficult to find a lawyer who specializes in the area of your legal problem. Keep that in mind if you ever decide to "let your fingers do the walking" through the Yellow Pages for a lawyer.

There is a related problem here. Lawyers who specialize in an area such as writing wills, do several a week. Their staff is proficient in getting the work out; computers or word processing equipment are programmed to quickly produce the product; and the result is that specialists can do the work for lower fees. However, in states where advertising of specialties is prohibited, the general practitioner can compete with the specialist because the latter cannot advertise a better product at a lower cost. If the specialist could advertise, then his volume would increase dramatically and the price of his services would come down. If it didn't, he would lose business to other specialists willing to cut their prices.

SUMMATION

In brief, few people know how to hire a decent lawyer. Furthermore, lack of legal internships and supervised specialization promotes incompetent and high-priced lawyers. The one who suffers is you, the client. The next three chapters will help you recognize the types of lawyers Justice Burger probably had in mind. The first are lawyers who share the same specialty: tricking clients.

2

Shysters

WEBSTER'S DICTIONARY defines the word "shyster" as a slang term, specifically, "a person, especially a lawyer, who uses unethical or tricky methods." While many lawyers equate the words "advocate" and "lawyer," few will equate the words "shyster" and "lawyer." Unfortunately, *Webster's* definition is a good one in many cases. Let's look at some examples of shysters—the types of lawyers you might get if you lose the lottery.

GREEDY LAWYERS

I once tried a divorce case against a shrewd divorce lawyer whose reputation for meanness in divorce cases got him a lot of business. My client was the husband, a wealthy man who had ditched his forty-five-year-old wife of twenty-odd years for a large-busted young lady. It was not a good case for my client, to put it mildly.

A few days before the trial, I met with the wife's lawyer to discuss settling the case. He seemed to be willing to negotiate everything but his fee, which he would be awarded by the court if the case were tried.

Taking note of this, I met with my client and told him that I felt we could get a favorable settlement, if he would agree to pay the excessive fee being demanded by his wife's lawyer. My client's first reaction was hostile. However, after I showed him that he would save in the settlement proposed many times the lawyer's fee, my client changed his mind.

I met again with the other lawyer and presented our offer. His eyes gleamed. His client, thinking she was represented by a real husband killer, bought his advice that our offer was a good one—hook, line, and sinker. She never knew what hit her. I later learned from other lawyers in the know that they had enjoyed the same experience with this lawyer—that while he often acted mean and did a lot of huffing and puffing, he could be had for a good fee any time.

If you are wondering why I took advantage of the unsuspecting wife in this fashion, it was what I was supposed to do as my client's lawyer—win. Now let's look at a close relative of the greedy lawyer.

HUNGRY LAWYERS

The hungry lawyer is not corrupt to the core like the greedy lawyer. Instead, he *behaves* corruptly because the wolf is at his door. Here's an example.

A friend of mine was a partner in a small law firm that had a cash flow problem—they weren't able to pay all of their bills. A new client came in to one of the other partners seeking help in buying a business. The sales price was $500,000 cash. The client had made a lot of money illegally and was trying to "launder" it (make it legitimate) by putting it into a legal business.

The partner took a $5,000 retainer at the first meeting with the client and began drawing up the purchase documents. Several days later, my friend learned about the new client. He also learned that the client had not been advised that the business purchase would be a red flag to the IRS. The latter would want to know where he had gotten the $500,000, since he had never paid income taxes on anywhere near that amount of income. Then, if the client was caught by the IRS for income tax evasion, he could have been prosecuted for the illegal activity that generated the $500,000. So, buying the business wasn't necessarily a smart thing for him to be doing.

My friend suggested to his partners that they explain all of this to the client and urge him to drop the whole idea. His partners' chief concern was having to return most of the $5,000 if the client decided not to go forward. A heated discussion followed, and the next day my friend resigned from the firm.

That same lawyer also told me that he knew of several instances where his firm had settled a good damage suit for less than it was worth, just to raise money to pay their bills—and themselves. I have, in fact, heard of this happening quite often. Of course, you won't hear about many cases like these, unless one of the lawyers involved talks. But often there are warning signs. Here's an example.

Several lawyers I know formed a new law partnership. Within a year, they purchased an old home and restored it, using variable rate financing—the kind that changes with interest rates. They borrowed about $400,000 for the project and initially were paying 9 percent interest. Then interest rates went to 21 percent. The law firm broke up; the lawyers moved to other locations; and it took three years to sell the empty building—and they all had to bring cash to the closing, because they didn't get enough from the sale to pay off the mortgage.

Those were hungry lawyers. I don't know if they ever did anything wrong to collect a fee, but knowing what I did about them, I never would have used them myself or referred a client to them. They just had too much besides being lawyers on their minds.

Money-grabbing lawyers are not the only types of shysters. Some simply aren't what they appear to be.

FAKES

One type of fake is the "boaster," the lawyer who acts as if he knows what he is doing, but really doesn't. Some lawyers are very skilled at fooling people, including other lawyers. Let me tell a story on myself.

When I first started practicing law—practice can be taken in its literal sense in this example—a young woman came to me with a real estate problem. She had been referred to me by a mutual friend who knew that I had handled some real estate matters.

The situation was this. My client had made an offer to buy an older home contingent on her getting an FHA loan. The lender had turned her down because of the poor condition of the home. Also, her credit was marginal. She really wanted the home, and sought my "expertise" to make the deal work. Her real estate agent, with vastly more experience than I, had been unable to help.

"You have nothing to worry about—I'm an FHA expert," I boasted. So she paid me a $500 retainer, and I started trying to learn something about FHA's appraisal and credit requirements. All to no avail, of course. In the end, the seller had to call off the deal and return my client's $1,000 earnest money deposit (binder), which she could have gotten back on her own. Of course, I didn't tell her that, and she left feeling that she had been well represented—glad to have her $500 (the $1,000 deposit less my $500 fee).

I am not proud of this story, but it demonstrates a common problem experienced with new or hungry lawyers. In my mind, I felt that I could help her. My eagerness to gain her business led me to stretch the truth about my capabilities at my client's expense. Many lawyers, unfortunately, misstate their expertise knowing full well that they will not be able to help the client.

There's another kind of fake—the "chicken fake." This type of shyster is usually quite knowledgeable about a given area of law, but is scared to death of certain parts of it—like trying cases. Take this example.

I know a lawyer who has a fabulous reputation for "working out" a certain type of criminal case. He boasts that he has never had a client go to prison, which is probably true. But all of the district attorneys know that this lawyer is terrified of trying a case—in fact, he's never tried one. And, when they plea bargain (negotiate) with him, the D.A.'s usually get him to agree to greater charges, larger fines, and longer probation sentences than many of his clients' cases warrant. In other words, he sells out his lesser or winnable cases in return for better than expected treatment on his tougher ones. This is how he keeps *all* of his clients from going to the penitentiary.

Another example is one of the better firms in my area, known for its tenacity in the early stages of a lawsuit. It inundates opposing lawyers with tons of paper—pleadings, interrogatories, depositions, pretrial hearings, and so forth. That often wears the opposition down, emotionally, financially or both. And all of that activity generates huge legal fees for the firm. However, if the other side can stick it out until trial date, then the worm turns, and the other side can get a very favorable settlement.

Here's why. Since that firm has collected most of its fee prior to trial—from all that paperwork, etc.—there is little economic incentive for it to go any further. More important, the firm prefers settlement to trial, because a trial carries the risk of losing the case, whereas a settlement does not, and the firm's image of not losing cases is primary to it. As a result, the firm leans on its clients to settle, not because the case is weak or because the settlement is favorable, but because it's in the firm's best interests that the case be settled.

There's a third kind of fake—the "inside fake." This type of shyster uses insider information (known only to lawyers) to make you think you are being represented, when, in fact, you are not. Take the following case.

For years in my state, any *first offender* charged with driving while intoxicated has been able to get the charge reduced to reckless driving by agreeing to go to defensive driver's school. That reduces the fine and saves the accused's driver's license. Many lay people do not know of this automatic reduction in the charge and routinely pay lawyers good money for "representing" them and "saving" their driver's license. The lawyers act as if they have done something wonderful; the clients are grateful and refer their drinking buddies to their lawyer, when they are stopped for drinking and driving, perpetuating the deception. I know several lawyers who make a very tidy income "negotiating" first-offender drunk driving charges.

Or take another situation. Several of the banks in my city have trust department lawyers who will draft wills and trusts, at no charge, for lawyers' clients. The hitch is that the client must agree to appoint the bank as executor of the estate and trustee of any trust(s) created. The documents are expertly prepared on a computer/word processor and look great. The client thinks the lawyer has done the work and gladly pays a fee far in excess of that justified by the real work performed by the lawyer. Then, when the client dies, the bank dutifully selects the lawyer's firm to handle the estate, for which it is paid a much larger legal fee than that charged initially. And the bank collects an even larger, additional fee as executor and trustee from the estate of a person it probably never did business with. Neat, huh?

There are other types of shysters who are also difficult to spot, such as the one with a "sue the bastards" mentality.

SUE THE BASTARDS

This lawyer is related to the bantam rooster—always wanting to fight: the other side and the other lawyer, too. When you go into this lawyer's office with your tale of woe and he starts telling you how great a case you have—that he's going to murder them—you will feel a lot better. Later, if you are perceptive, you will realize that this lawyer doesn't know how to do anything but fight, and that not very well either. His emotions prevent him from thinking or being intuitive, and you get the short end of it.

A relative of the suit-happy lawyer is the "fee generator."

FEE GENERATORS

This is the lawyer who is more interested in running up his fee than in solving your problem.

A woman I know was getting a divorce. She and her husband had tried to divvy everything up, and his lawyer drew up the divorce agreement. She carried it to another lawyer to review. This second lawyer told her that she was giving up too much—that he could get her a lot more. Not knowing any better, she let him represent her.

In the end, she got almost exactly what she had initially agreed to take, less, of course, a whopping legal fee. Her husband ended up having to pay his lawyer a lot, too. In fact, the total legal fees were about ten times what the first lawyer would have charged for drawing up the agreement to which my friend and her husband had originally agreed.

Then there's the lawyer who will say anything you want to hear to get and keep you as a client. This is the "Dale Carnegie" lawyer.

DALE CARNEGIES

First, let me say I use this analogy in jest. I have taken several Dale Carnegie courses, worked with others as a "graduate assistant" in such courses, and one of my best friends is the Dale Carnegie sponsor in my city. I admire the organization and the things it teaches. However, the Dale Carnegie techniques can be abused by manipulative people, and the "Dale Carnegie" lawyer is very skilled in applying those techniques to snow you, as opposed to sincerely winning your friendship. The "Dale Carnegie" lawyer will not argue with you or do anything to ruffle your feathers. In other words, this type of shyster is not an "adviser advocate." As that term is defined in Chapter 6, an adviser advocate is a lawyer who will argue with you at the risk of making you mad—even at the risk of you firing him because you do not like his candid advice.

Another sneaky shyster is the "diplomat."

DIPLOMATS

Behavior typical of the "diplomat" lawyer is described in the following example.

A lawyer I know reads the daily obituaries. Whenever he sees the name of anyone he knows—or even the close friend or relative of anyone he knows—he marks the funeral date on his calendar.

He may write a letter of condolence, depending on how well he knows the people involved, or he may call them on the telephone. He then goes to the funeral, signs the register, and tries to stand where the bereaved friend or relative can see him. At the conclusion of the ceremony, he offers his sympathy and legal assistance. Nice guy, huh?

There's another type of "solicitor" who is less obvious. This shyster is more closely related to the pure "ambulance chaser"—the lawyer who comes to visit you in the hospital after you've just been involved in a terrible automobile accident that wasn't your fault.

CLOSET AMBULANCE CHASERS

This type won't come to see you in the hospital. Instead, you will be given the lawyer's business card by a police officer at the scene of the accident, by the paramedics who drive you in the ambulance to the hospital or by one of the hospital's staff. They then call the lawyer, explain your case and give your name. If you use that lawyer, he sends them a "present," which could be more than you make a week.

THE DEADBEAT

The "deadbeat" lawyer takes you on as a client, then never does anything. For example, a client of mine operated a woodworking company. She did some work for a contractor but he refused to pay her bill of $1,800. So she went to a lawyer "friend," who told her she had an open-and-shut case and that he would get on it as soon as she paid the $40 filing fee for the lawsuit. She wrote him a check on the spot and left feeling great.

During the next several months, the lawyer made several "progress" reports to her and told her of three different trial dates—each being continued at the last minute for reasons unexplained. Finally, she came to me, as I had represented her on several other matters in the past. I went to the courthouse and looked at the court records. The case had been filed only three weeks earlier—some five months after she had paid the filing fee. A trial date had never been set. I called the lawyer to see if there was another side to the story. There wasn't. I suggested that he get the case over with as soon as possible. He didn't. So I advised my client to file a grievance against him. She did, and he was brought to task before the grievance committee—and reprimanded.

MADISON AVENUE LAWYERS

Then there's the shyster who does a lot of advertising to get business. This is the lawyer you typically see on TV or hear on radio doing his own tasteless commercials. Sometimes you see his ads in the newspaper. The ads go something like this: "Need a lawyer, call me"; "If you've been injured in an accident, call me first"; and so forth. My general view of this type of lawyer is that he's not good enough to get business the normal way, that is, by referrals from fellow lawyers or satisfied clients who know of his skills. On the other hand, if the lawyer offers a uniquely helpful service, such as being bilingual in an ethnic community, or offers an efficient, low-cost legal clinic or specialty, then this information should be made known to the public by whatever means available. In such cases, tasteful, informative advertising is appropriate.

BAIT-AND-SWITCHERS

Closely related to the Madison Avenue shyster is the bait-and-switch lawyer. Often, but not always, this lawyer uses advertising or some other come on gimmick to get you into his office, then he talks you into letting him do a lot more than you think you need. Let's look at some examples.

Lawyer Sly advertises $49 cut-rate, uncontested divorces. You and your spouse have everything all worked out and go in to get it over with. That's when you learn that $49 covers the divorce but not your agreement. That will be another $150. And by the way, now that you're getting divorced, don't you need new wills? Or, wouldn't you like to go bankrupt and get all of those creditors off your back?

Take another situation. You go to a lawyer to help you get worker's compensation or social security disability benefits. He gets them for you, but his fee is low because it is made so by statute. So he suggests that you and your spouse need wills (or new ones).

Or this case. A lawyer advertises that for only $25 he can get your creditors to stop hounding you. He gets you to sign a damage suit agreement authorizing him to sue the creditors for illegal harassment. Then he gets a $7,500 settlement and the offending creditor(s) forgive what you owe.

All of the above examples are bait-and-switch cases. You are invited in for one thing and get something else. Many lawyers do business that way on a regular basis. You aren't always injured, because you probably need a will if you don't have one. And splitting that $7,500 with the lawyer and getting your creditors off your back is certainly an improvement over your situation. However, a first-rate damage suit lawyer might have been able to recover $25,000. Just be aware of what is going on and be prepared to say "no" when you should.

SUMMATION

As you can see, there are more types of shysters than meet the eye.
The bar associations and lawyer licensing agencies eventually weed
out the flagrant ones: the pure ambulance chasers and those who steal
their clients' money, work in league with the other side, seduce their
emotionally distressed divorce clients, charge fees for work never
done, or those who are habitual drunks or drug addicts. The less
obvious shysters, such as the varieties described in this chapter, are
more difficult to spot and can be extremely costly to use. The ways to
avoid them are described in Chapter 7. But avoiding shysters is not
the only problem you face in hiring a competent lawyer. Further
problems arise when lawyers try to serve two masters—as will be
seen in the next chapter.

3

Double Dealers

THE ADMONITION OF Matthew 6:24 that "No man can serve two masters" is as appropriate with lawyers as with anyone else. Indeed, you would probably be better off in the hands of any of the shysters you met in the preceding chapter than in the hands of a double agent. Let's look at some examples and see why.

THE BUSINESS'S LAWYER

A man once came to me for help with his estate plan. He owned a very profitable business that he was buying from its retired founder. On looking through the documents which my client had brought in, I found two agreements allowing him to purchase the business from the founder. The first agreement, prepared by the company lawyer some ten years earlier, gave my client a minority interest in the company and the right to purchase the remainder of it within eight years for $125,000. The second agreement, executed eight years later, raised the price to $325,000 but otherwise was the same as the first agreement.

My curiosity aroused, I asked my client why he had agreed to pay more when he didn't have to do it. His reply was that the business had done better than expected (thanks to his efforts), and the founder came to regret the first agreement. So, the founder instructed the company lawyer to draw up the new agreement and make my client sign it. The lawyer told my client that he would have to sign the new agreement, and my client, who trusted the lawyer and didn't want to make waves (which the lawyer knew), signed it.

The lawyer was in a classic conflict-of-interest position. First, he represented the business and had a primary duty to protect it. Second, he had done legal work for both my client and the founder (the first agreement) and had on that occasion represented both of them. Third, he later took sides with the founder, which action either risked damage to the business (if a fight ensued) or injury to my client. The real crime, however, was that the lawyer "did in" my client knowing that my client trusted him to do what was right.

The lawyer either should have declined to draw up the new agreement or should have advised my client that he did not have to sign it and to seek another lawyer's advice before doing so. Of course, the lawyer, not wishing to lose the founder's favor, didn't do this. And my client lost $200,000 as a result.

THE WILL WRITER

Another very common conflict-of-interest area is writing and enforcing wills. Almost every lawyer will write a client's will at some time or another. Then, when the client dies, the family will return to that lawyer to wind up the decedent's estate. Having written the will, the lawyer is now charged with the task of enforcing it. There are several interesting conflicts that can develop here.

What if there is an ambiguous phrase in the will such as "I leave everything to my beloved wife, Nellie, during life." Does this mean Nellie gets it all, or just the right to use it during her life? If the latter, who gets it when she dies? Suppose there is an estranged son who wants his share when Nellie dies, and Nellie doesn't like that. What's the lawyer to do? He drew the will and knows what the decedent really wanted, but he goofed it up by not specifying what would happen when Nellie died. The best thing for the lawyer to do is to resign from handling the estate so that he can testify without any conflict. He should also call his malpractice carrier and advise that either Nellie or the estranged son may be considering a malpractice action.

Suppose instead that Nellie was the decedent's second wife, and she got everything to the exclusion of her husband's children by his first wife. The kids won't be very happy about that and will probably hire their own lawyer to prove that Nellie, with the help of "her" lawyer, coerced the decedent into disinheriting his children. That puts the first lawyer in the uncomfortable position of having to defend the will—rather than the estate and heirs—not only to protect his reputation but to keep the estate itself as a client. For if the will is ruled to be invalid, the lawyer who drew it has lost a client.

Another problem that could arise is who gets what. Suppose the decedent left half to Nellie, half to his children. Assume further that one-third of the estate is real estate and two-thirds stocks, bonds, and cash. What if everyone wants the liquid assets? Or what if the land was Grandfather Leopold's farm? Nellie lives on it, but the kids want it. Who decides the allocation? Why wasn't it spelled out in the will? Again, the lawyer is in an uncomfortable position and should resign. Fat chance of that happening, however.

THE CLOSING ATTORNEY

Now let's look at what happens when you buy a home. In many areas, a lawyer will handle the closing. He prepares your deed, takes your money and pays the seller, the real estate agent (if any), and a myriad of other bills. If you are borrowing money to buy the home, the lawyer prepares the loan documents, all of which are grossly unfair to you, and you pay the lawyer for doing it.

If a real estate agent is involved, then the lawyer was probably chosen by the agent. In fact, the agent probably sends the lawyer closings on a regular basis, and the lawyer reciprocates with home buyer and seller referrals to the agent. Perhaps the lawyer even represents the agent personally, or the agent's real estate firm.

What does the lawyer do if a problem develops between you and the seller? Suppose the sales contract says the seller will pay up to $2,000 of the closing costs, but closing costs are $3,000. Who pays the overage? The contract doesn't say.

Since the agent drew up the contract, perhaps the agent should pay for the unresolved costs. But the agent sends the lawyer business, and the lawyer's not about to suggest such a thing. If the lawyer sides with you against the seller, the agent (who represents the seller) may get mad; so will the seller. If the lawyer sides with the seller, you will get upset, especially if you are paying the lawyer's fee. If the lawyer doesn't collect the $1,000, the lending company will be upset. Whom does this lawyer represent? It's difficult to say, isn't it?

"WE BOTH HAD THE SAME LAWYER"

Two people having the same lawyer happens often in divorce cases. The spouses feel that they have everything resolved and want to save money on legal fees. Some of the worst results I've ever seen have come out of this situation. Invariably, the lawyer will subtly take sides. In fact, in most states, the lawyer cannot represent both sides without the spouses agreeing to such an arrangement in writing and before the lawyer does any work. Many times I've heard someone say, "My wife took me to the cleaners," or "I have three children and that lout—my ex-husband—only has to pay me $200 a month in support." Without even asking, I know that the odds are that the complainer shared a lawyer with her (or his) spouse.

SUMMATION

The acid test for determining whether or not there is a conflict of interest is to look at who is involved in your case. Ask yourself if you are in any kind of dispute with them, or if it's possible that you might be later. If the answer to either question is "yes," the lawyer is a double agent and cannot be trusted to protect you against that person. It's that simple.

Now let's look at another area where you can get hurt—when lawyers work together.

4

The Lawyer Brotherhood

IT'S AN UNDENIABLE fact that there is a good deal of clubbishness among lawyers and judges. In this chapter we are going to look at some of the ways that clubbishness can lead to problems. First, let's look at what I have found to be an almost universal concern of people who have had unpleasant dealings with lawyers.

"MY LAWYER SOLD ME OUT"

I can't recall the number of times that I have heard someone say, "I thought I had a good case, but my lawyer and the other side's lawyer got together in private and I got sold down the river." Well, I'm sad to say that this does happen. Take the case I overheard in the lawyers' coffee room in a courthouse.

Two lawyers at the table had been waiting all morning to try a small damage suit. They had just learned that their case would not be called until after lunch, although it had been set on the morning's trial docket. One of the lawyers said, "Hell, I'm not getting paid enough on this case to stay up here all day!" The other lawyer chimed in, "Nor am I; let's settle this thing and get back to the office where we can make some money." And that is exactly what they did, even though both clients wanted a trial. They simply told their respective clients that the other side had made a very reasonable offer that should be accepted, or risk defeat and get nothing. The clients, feeling that they had no alternatives, agreed to the settlement.

That example presents a common dilemma. Not all lawyers are like those two, but even good lawyers usually do not like to have their clients present during the negotiating process. Why? Because few clients are capable of negotiating anything, much less their own case. Countless times, clients have lost out in the negotiations because they would not hang in there and wait out the other side. Or, they gave away their position—their anxiousness—and the other side waited them out. So, if you allow your lawyer to negotiate out of your presence, you risk the result given in the example. If you attend the negotiations, you risk botching them yourself.

Of course, you do not have to accept a settlement negotiated by your lawyer, and you are fully entitled to question him about it or insist on a trial. On the other hand, not accepting the settlement that your lawyer recommends is a judgment call on your part, and most people are not sophisticated enough to make such decisions. That is why it is crucial to select a competent, ethical lawyer at the very beginning. (How to do that is discussed in Chapter 7.)

If you select a good lawyer, then I would not worry about being sold out, even if you see your lawyer walking down the hall arm-in-arm with the other side's lawyer. Lawyers are people, too, meaning that they have lawyer friends and enjoy activities away from the office with each other. Many lawyers have friendships with each other dating back to law school, or even before that. Often they work on the same bar committees together or have offices in the same building. So, it should be no surprise that some of them are chummy with each other.

Many times I have seen lawyers playing racquetball at the YMCA, during lunch hour or after work. It kills them to lose the game, and the winners tease the losers unmercifully. That afternoon or the next day, they are at each other's throats in the court room, fighting just as hard as they did on the courts. When it's over, they are still friends, just as they were after the racquetball game was over. The trick is to select a good lawyer; then you won't have to worry about his friendships.

Now let's look at another clubby trait of lawyers that can be very frustrating if your lawyer has botched your case.

LEGAL MALPRACTICE SUITS

I recently was called upon by another law firm to evaluate a real estate case, an area in which I now specialize. Without getting too involved in the facts, let me say that one thing I found and advised them of was that the closing lawyer had acted negligently and should be made a defendant in the lawsuit already in progress. The plaintiff's lawyer agreed with my opinion but stated that he just couldn't sue another lawyer, because his firm got the bulk of its cases as referrals *from other lawyers*. The lawyer said that he would advise his client of the malpractice possibility and that if his client wanted to sue the closing lawyer, he would resign from the case. I never was told what actually happened.

In another case, a young lawyer unwisely filed a flimsy lawsuit against a doctor. The case had been referred to the lawyer by another law firm that represented a lot of doctors. Of course, the other firm was afraid of angering its other doctor clients by bringing the lawsuit. Nevertheless, it insisted on a "referral" fee out of any recovery that might be made.

The young lawyer filed the lawsuit, and before long it became obvious that the doctor was innocent and would win. After consulting with his client, the lawyer approached the doctor's lawyer and offered to dismiss the case. The doctor's lawyer suggested, instead, that they let the court dismiss it on the ground that the statute of limitations had run before the suit was filed. (The statute of limitations was an issue in the case.) That, he said, would avoid an admission by the young lawyer or his client that they had filed a frivolous lawsuit. Otherwise, the doctor would be in a position to sue for abusive litigation. As you can imagine, the young lawyer quickly agreed to his suggestion. Note that the doctor's lawyer destroyed the case his client would have had against the young lawyer and his client, all in an effort to protect another lawyer.

Ten years ago, it would have been very difficult to find a lawyer willing to sue another lawyer. And it's still difficult today. (In Chapter 14, you will learn how to find such a lawyer if you need one.)

Now let's look at another cozy relationship, which was raised briefly in the last example.

THE REFERRAL FEE

Often a lawyer gets a case that he doesn't know how to handle or have the time to do so. When that happens, the lawyer will refer the case to a "specialist," a lawyer who regularly handles that type of case. Typically, the specialist will agree to remit a "referral" or "forwarding" fee to the referring lawyer. Usually illegal, this type of fee splitting is nevertheless common practice and often adds substantially to the legal costs. The amount of the referral fee can vary from, say, 10 to 50 percent of the fee the specialist ultimately collects—all of which comes out of your pocket. Often the client is never advised of this arrangement, or if he is, of the fact that the forwarding lawyer will do little, if any, work on the case.

For example, a lawyer I know was asked by a family to handle the estate of a deceased relative. During the first meeting with his clients, the lawyer learned that the decedent had been killed in an automobile accident that was not his fault. It was an excellent damage suit, in other words, and the clients, for reasons of their own, were totally unaware of this fact. The lawyer got his clients to sign a contract employing him or any firm he chose to handle the case for 50 percent of the recovery. Then he walked them down the street and introduced them to a large plaintiff's firm. The referral fee arrangement was fifty-fifty between the lawyer and the plaintiff's firm.

Ultimately, the case was settled for $400,000 and the lawyer thus pocketed $100,000 for half a day's work. Granted that but for him, his clients might never have gotten anything. But $100,000? By the way, the $100,000 fee to the plaintiff's firm was fully earned. Its reputation for obtaining large judgments contributed substantially to the large settlement and avoided "the hazards of litigation" discussed in Chapter 11.

COURT REFERRALS

Now let's look back at the driving-while-intoxicated case mentioned in Chapter 3, to see how judges often help lawyers make unnecessary fees.

The driving-while-intoxicated case concerned lawyers who obtain "automatic" reductions in criminal charges while acting as if they are doing something wonderful. For several years, our local courts helped this along by refusing to hear DWI cases when the accused was not represented by a lawyer. This, of course, made it impossible for the accused to handle his own "automatic" reduction case, even if he knew how to do it.

Or take this scenario. To get your name legally changed in many courts, all you have to do is fill out a preprinted form, stating your old and new names and mailing address, sign it, get it notarized, and have the judge sign and record it. For several years in my city, those forms were available, just by asking for them, at the courthouse. Then the local lawyers complained and the practice was stopped. Now, even lay people who know what's involved are told they must get a lawyer to do it. Simple tasks such as these are where the "how to be your own lawyer" books may come in handy—if only to help you negotiate the lawyer's fee. (More on that topic in Chapter 8.)

JUDGES CAN DO NO WRONG

Judges, who are usually lawyers, are members of the club, too. The following, amusing case explains this phenomenon. It was told to me in my favorite place to meet other lawyers, the steamroom at the YMCA.

A lawyer friend was handling a divorce case, representing the husband. They knew the identities of *several* of the wife's lovers and had charged her with adultery in the divorce suit, offering by a thinly veiled threat to prove the identities of the various men she had been seeing. One of them was a respected local judge.

About three weeks before the trial, my friend subpoenaed all of the lovers to appear as witnesses at the trial, including the judge. Immediately, my friend was called by several respected lawyers, each of whom questioned his trial tactics without specifically asking him to cancel the judge's subpoena. My friend knew that by subpoenaing the judge he would get such calls but he also knew that a lot of pressure would also be put on the wife to settle out of court for much less than she might otherwise get. Adultery isn't all that big a deal in the courts anymore, but the embarrassment of a respected and married judge still is.

Well, my friend asked the other lawyers what exactly did they want him to do: sell out his own client? Of course, none would come out and say, "Let the judge go." So he asked them to send him a letter explaining what they wanted so that he could take it up with his client. That, of course, was the end of the pressure on his side of the suit, but just the beginning, no doubt, of the problems for the wife's lawyer. In the end, the case settled on terms very favorable to my friend's client.

The point to that story is this: Most lawyers will do anything they can to protect a judge from the law. By doing so, they hope to receive favorable treatment in their future cases before him.

JUDGES PROTECT LAWYERS, TOO

There's another side to the lawyer/judge mutual admiration society. Time and time again, I've seen cases where lawyers (including me) let

something fall through the cracks, only to be bailed out by a sympathetic judge. Having once been lawyers themselves, judges feel for
lawyers in these situations. However, the result often is detrimental
to one of the clients and contrary to a judge's theoretically impartial
position.

For example, a friend of mine was owed about $2,500 and couldn't
collect it. He went to a lawyer, who brought a lawsuit to collect the
money. The defendant didn't respond to the suit papers, and the
lawyer took a default judgment for $2,500 against the defendant.
After the time for filing an appeal (see Chapter 14) passed, my friend's
lawyer sent the defendant a letter advising that a garnishment on the
defendant's employer and bank accounts would be filed if the money
wasn't paid. Once served with the garnishment notice, the defendant's employer or bank would have to turn over to the court any
moneys they owed the defendant or had on deposit for him, up to
$2,500.

The next day, a new lawyer filed a motion before the judge asking
that the case be reopened. His grounds were that his client (the
defendant) had sent him the suit papers and he had somehow lost
them and had not, therefore, responded to my friend's lawsuit. The
judge knew that the defendant's lawyer would have to pay the judgment out of his own pocket—even if the defendant owed the
money—because the defendant never had his day in court. So the
judge reopened the case. Furthermore, my friend's lawyer, also in
sympathy with defendant's lawyer, did not oppose reopening the
case, even though it was in his client's interest to do so. For if the case
were not reopened, the defendant would have had to pay the
$2,500—even if he didn't owe it.

In another example, a very fine defense lawyer failed to file income tax returns for several years. No excuse. He just didn't do it.
Eventually, the IRS came knocking, and he was indicted for income
tax evasion. Besides facing a stiff fine and prison sentence, he was certain to lose his law license if convicted. The U.S. attorney and U.S.
district judge allowed the lawyer to enter a special kind of plea to the
charges called *nolo contendere*, meaning, "I don't admit or deny the
charges." A *nolo* conviction is not considered a criminal conviction.
That saved him from prison and losing his law license. The fine wasn't
much either. If it had been you instead of a lawyer? Good luck!

Now let's look at an area of the brotherhood dear to the hearts of
all lawyers.

THE LEGAL ECONOMIC CARTEL

Lawyers don't like competition from nonlawyers, or anything else that adversely affects their revenues. They go to extremes in many cases to protect their pocketbooks, at your expense, of course. We've already seen an illustration of this, in the change-of-name example earlier in this chapter. Here are some others.

For years local bar associations printed and distributed minimum fee guidelines for lawyers to use in setting fees. Adherence to those guidelines was "encouraged," and lawyers were able to point to the guidelines to justify fees and inability to negotiate same. A few well-placed antitrust price-fixing suits stopped this open client-gouging practice. However, many lawyers still pay very close attention to what their competition is charging. Sometimes they even have secret meetings and discuss their fees. You can beat this practice by shopping around.

Another example involves a lady named Rosemary Furman who, after many years of legal secretarial experience, opened a "self-help" legal clinic in Jacksonville, Florida. She gave out a lot of change-of-name-type forms and other very basic be-your-own-lawyer advice. The bar associations and courts crushed her for the unauthorized practice of law. The sad thing was that, while Furman was technically guilty of giving "legal" advice, she was helping only those people whose cases did not really need the services of a lawyer. The beneficiaries of her being put out of business, if any, were the local lawyers who weren't competent to handle anything more complex than a change-of-name case, something that any lawyer's secretary can do any day of the week.

Another way lawyers protect their pocketbooks is in the area of lawyer advertising. The Federal Trade Commission has found that in states where there are few restrictions on lawyers advertising, fees invariably are lower. That's the real reason that the bar associations are fighting so hard to restrict lawyer advertising—to protect you from lower legal fees, not shysters!

Here's another one. I once tried to set up a not-for-profit public interest real estate law firm. Not wanting to go out and spend a lot of time begging for donations, preferring instead to do law work, I decided to try to predominantly fund the firm by charging clients on an ability-to-pay basis. The poor would get free representation, the more fortunate would pay on a sliding scale related to income. Then I discovered an IRS revenue ruling prohibiting tax-exempt public law firms from charging fees, other than those that might be awarded from the other side by statute. That left me with either spending most of my time asking for donations or operating on a profit basis. I chose the second approach.

Later I learned from *Public Citizen* magazine, founded by Ralph Nader, that the American Bar Association (ABA) had lobbied the IRS to pass that revenue ruling, I guess to discourage public interest law firms, such as the Legal Services Corporation, which tend to bring antiestablishment types of lawsuits. The ABA is, of course, about as conservative an organization as you can find. If that revenue ruling were revoked, public interest law firms would not be so clearly at the mercy of government funding cutbacks, the poor might be able to obtain legal services on a regular basis, and the legal economic cartel would be a little less rich.

My last lawyer economics lesson should raise some eyebrows. Suppose you get mad at your lawyer and want to fire him and get another lawyer to handle your case. So you tell him off and ask for your file. Don't hold your breath. The lawyer has the right to keep your file until you have paid him in full, or until he has agreed to be paid later. This right, called the "lawyer's lien," was created, of course, by lawyers. The only time the lien does not apply is when the lawyer has botched your case or has acted unethically toward you— something that you may have trouble proving.

DISCRIMINATION

There's one more area of the brotherhood that needs addressing. I hope women readers will forgive me for using "he" throughout this book to refer to the lawyer. Sexist though the term may be, the fact remains that most practicing lawyers are men.

If you don't believe that the brotherhood discriminates against women lawyers, just go out and take a head count of the women in private practice in your area. As a former blue-ribbon, male chauvinist pig, I speak with authority on this one.

I know a woman lawyer, and a damn good one, too, who worked for a local, prestigious law firm for several years. Each year, she came up for a partnership consideration. Each time, she was told, "Not this year." Finally, a friend on the promotion committee leveled with her: "Not any year." They then smoothed it over by getting her hired as inside counsel for the large bank they represented. She was so good that she took a lot of their work away from them and now often decides what, if anything, they will do for the bank. Yay!

The sad point of this subsection is that it's still pretty much a man's world in the lawyer arena. All of this will eventually change for the better, but it hasn't yet. The same applies for racial and ethnic discrimination, too. Until these changes occur, it will be more difficult than it should be for you to find a female or minority lawyer with whom you will be happy.

SUMMATION

I hope this and the first three chapters turned on some lights for you. The problems presented are generally not known to lay people, and you can bet that few lawyers will tell you about them. Why? Because, according to Justice Burger, a majority of the lawyers in our country have been described in these chapters, thus they would be telling on themselves. That behind us, let's turn our attention to the relationship between you and your lawyer-to-be.

PART II

THE LAWYER-CLIENT RELATIONSHIP

5

When to Go to a Lawyer

NEXT TO PICKING one of the bad lawyers described in Part I, not knowing if you need a lawyer or waiting too long to see one when you need legal help are the two biggest mistakes a potential client can make. Therefore, the first order of business here is to learn when you need a lawyer.

If you ever need a lawyer's services, it probably will be in one of the following general areas:

Friendly Matters. Writing a will, adopting a child, probating the estate of a deceased relative, forming a new corporation, drawing up a partnership or buy-sell agreement, buying or selling a home, and so forth.

Advisory Situations. When you are thinking about doing something or are concerned about something happening. For example, going into business with someone else, making a real estate investment, setting up a trust to protect your family when you die, saving taxes, avoiding a debt, going bankrupt, getting divorced, and so forth.

Distress Zones. When you are already in trouble and know it. For example, you were at fault in an automobile accident, you were injured in an automobile accident that was not your fault, your creditors are hounding you, you have been sued for a divorce, you are charged with committing a serious crime, your social security benefits have been terminated, and so forth.

Let's look at each of these in a little more detail. In friendly situations, you generally aren't under much pressure to act, so you can pretty much choose when to seek a lawyer's help. However, putting off attending to even a friendly legal matter can sometimes be devastating. For instance, if you die without a will, your estate probably will not pass to your heirs as you wished (or as they expected).

33

Furthermore, the legal fees required of an intestate (no will) estate generally will far exceed those of a testate (with a will) estate.

The advisory situations are gray areas—where you may not yet *need* a lawyer, but where you feel that a lawyer's advice *might* be helpful. Nevertheless, you're reluctant to talk to a lawyer because of the cost. Or, perhaps you simply don't go to lawyers unless you are in a distress zone? This is the area that causes the most problems and will be discussed shortly in depth.

When you are in a distress zone, you *know* that you need a lawyer and, hopefully, won't put off seeing one. Unless it's a small claims court matter (discussed in Chapter 16), you probably should not try to handle a distress zone case yourself, or, in lawyer jargon, *pro se.* The saying "He who has himself for a lawyer has a fool for a client" can apply here with a vengeance. For instance, suppose you are injured in an automobile accident and are not at fault. It takes you several months to fully recover from your injuries. The other driver's insurance adjuster has asked you to give him a chance to settle out of court with you before you hire a lawyer. That seemed reasonable, so you did not get a lawyer. But when the adjuster made his offer, it was lower than you felt it should be (as it usually is). You stew over the situation for a while, then decide to hire a lawyer. Unfortunately, by this time, the automobiles have been repaired without any extent-of-damage pictures having been taken, or a key eyewitness in your favor has moved to parts unknown, or the statute of limitations for filing suit has run out.

Now let's go back to the advisory situation area. That is a planning or, if you will, a preventive stage. You aren't in trouble yet, but soon could be. Perhaps a lawyer can steer you around the trouble and keep you out of a distress zone. Two popular sayings apply here: "An ounce of prevention is worth a pound of cure," and "The horse is out of the barn." From the lawyer's viewpoint, another saying covers both situations: "You can pay me now, or you can pay me later."

I assure you that it costs a lot more to get the horse back in the barn than it does to keep him there. And often the horse, once loose, can't be found at any cost. In other words, it invariably pays to head problems off at the pass. Let's leave the analogies and look at some real cases that demonstrate what I mean.

"BUT I DIDN'T DO ANYTHING WRONG!"

A young couple sold their home. The sales contract drawn up by the real estate agents stated that the house was *not* located in a flood plain. Unknown to the couple, it was. It was the agents' job to determine that before drawing up the contract. In fact, a simple telephone call to city hall would have gotten the correct information. So the agents fouled up.

After the closing, an unprecedented rain came, leaving the home surrounded by water with the buyers trapped inside. Not surprisingly, they were a mite upset. They got more upset later when their lawyer told them that their home was located in a flood plain. The sellers became equally as upset when the sheriff served the suit papers.

The sellers realized that they were in a distress zone and hired me to defend the case. It was my sad duty to inform them that they had no defense to the suit, for two reasons. First, the agents had been employed by my clients. Therefore, my clients were liable to the buyers for any negligent acts or omissions of the agents, who indeed had been negligent in not determining the true flood plain status. Second, by accepting the contract stating that the property was not located in a flood plain, my clients had misrepresented (albeit innocently) the true facts. They were, therefore, liable to the buyers for having made an "innocent" misrepresentation.

My clients were morally, but not legally, innocent. It probably had never dawned on them to seek a lawyer's advice before signing the contract. If they had brought it to me before signing it, I would have checked the flood plain status. For about $50, they could have saved several thousand dollars in legal fees and the torment and risk of a lengthy and dangerous lawsuit, the outcome of which is still in the air.

In the next case, I think that my client knew better, but was too tightfisted to hire a lawyer.

PENNY-WISE AND POUND-FOOLISH

My client, an accountant, decided to buy a house as an investment. He found one with a garage apartment, which the real estate agent told him could be rented out. He ran the numbers and determined that, by renting out both the house and the apartment, the deal would make a pretty good investment. He borrowed a lot of money and bought the property.

A few weeks later, after renting both units, he went down to the power company to have a separate meter put on the apartment. By doing that, he would have been able to charge each renter separately for their power usage. To his shock, he was told that it couldn't be done because the apartment was no longer legal under the zoning laws.

Instead of leaving well enough alone and quietly renting the garage apartment, he decided to play lawyer in earnest by filing a petition for a zoning variance. This, of course, tipped off the city officials to his illegal apartment, and his petition was denied at the zoning hearing. Realizing he was now in a distress zone, he came to me.

Unfortunately, he took too long doing it. By the time I first met with him, the fifteen-day statute of limitations for appealing the zoning ruling had run out, so there was nothing that I could do to remedy the zoning problem. My advice was that he secretly rent the apartment and consider suing the seller and real estate agent for innocent misrepresentation. That didn't go down well, as the seller was an eighty-year-old woman living in a nursing home and the agent was a friend of his. He tried to continue renting the apartment, but the city shut him down. When that happened, he reluctantly engaged me to file the lawsuit.

Again, a simple telephone call to city hall would have disclosed the zoning problem and kept that miserable tale out of this book. Now let's look at another area where the unsuspecting wander into distress zones.

"WE BOTH USED THE SAME LAWYER"

This subject was touched on in Chapter 3, where my client paid $200,000 too much for his business. You can be sure that he kicks himself every time he makes a mortgage payment on a loan that would have been paid in full long ago, had he sought a second lawyer's advice *before* signing the new agreement.

Remember that I also suggested in Chapter 3 that using the same lawyer in a divorce case might prove unrewarding. Take the kind of divorce where everything is "all worked out." I've been called many times by people wanting to know what I would charge for an "uncontested" divorce—one where everything was resolved and all I was to do was draw up the papers. The fact is that only about 10 percent of those cases were really "all worked out," and I invariably had to get involved in negotiating a final agreement.

That leads me to an important point: You can't both have the *same* lawyer in a divorce. He has to represent one of you, because that's the way the system is set up. Consider yourself to be in a distress zone whenever you are getting a divorce. At least have another lawyer look over the agreement before you sign it. Here's why.

Once a divorce agreement has been approved by the court, it's all over but the crying. The only way to get the agreement changed against the wishes of your ex is to hire a lawyer, go back to court, and prove either that your condition has substantially worsened or that your ex's condition has materially improved *since the date* that the court approved the agreement.

If your reason for wanting to get the agreement changed is that you simply miscalculated what you could afford to pay in support (or what support you would need), then you are out of luck. The horse is out of the barn and long gone. The money you "saved" using the same lawyer will amount to peanuts in comparison with what you now face paying (or not getting paid). If, instead, your motive for using his (or her) lawyer was just to get the thing over with as quickly and as painlessly as possible, you will hate yourself for not hanging in there and negotiating a better settlement. I could give you about a hundred examples of this and so could any other lawyer who does divorce work.

A general word of caution here. If you ask for a lawyer's advice about a settlement agreement drawn up by your spouse's lawyer, you will be smart to tell him that his advice is all that you are seeking. If you don't do this, you risk ending up with a "fee generator" for a lawyer (see Chapter 2). That, remember, is the type of lawyer who will tell you to reject the settlement, even though it's reasonable, so that he can make a larger fee by representing you in the divorce suit.

THE COAL MINER'S SLAUGHTER

The owner of a successful insurance agency contacted me to file suit against a partner of his in a coal mining venture. Two years previously the partner, a small coal miner, had approached the insurance agent with a proposition. The coal miner had mining experience and title to considerable coal mining equipment (bulldozers, front-end loaders, etc.). He also had coal leases. He had heard that the insurance agent had, in short, money. The proposal was that the coal miner contribute his equipment, leases, and experience, and that the insurance agent contribute money, and they go into the coal mining business. A corporation was formed, and they did so.

Unknown to the insurance agent, and possibly even to the coal miner, it is almost never feasible to mine coal with rolling equipment only. A large machine called a dragline is usually necessary to be competitive. Accordingly, the venture did not work out, and the insurance agent began to suspect the coal miner of chicanery. He contacted me to determine his rights.

Unfortunately, when "their" attorney (they used the coal miner's attorney) "incorporated" them, he did not draw up a bill of sale of the coal miner's equipment to the new corporation or an assignment of the coal miner's leases to the corporation. On the other hand, he did have them open a bank account in the new corporation's name and deposited the insurance agent's money ($50,000) in the account. The corporation thereby immediately got, so to speak, title to the money, but not to the equipment or the leases. Thus, when the insurance agent approached the coal miner with his grievances, the latter's comment was, "We have spent your money and need some more. I have the equipment and the leases still in my name. If you don't like it, sue me."

The corporation had, of course, a good claim to the equipment and leases. But a good claim means, essentially, that after three or four years of fencing in court, it could get the equipment and leases. Perhaps. But not in this case. We filed suit, and the coal miner went bankrupt, which left us standing in line with his many other creditors.

I suggested on one occasion that the insurance agent might consider making a claim against the attorney for a conflict of interest. He shrugged his shoulders and said he did not think so because the attorney was "a nice guy." He did, however, indicate considerable bitterness about the $2,500 retainer I had charged to file his unsuccessful suit.

Before concluding this chapter, I would like to relate a success story about a client who headed off a serious problem at the pass.

A STITCH IN TIME SAVES NINE

In this case, the parents of a teenage girl came to a lawyer I know for consultation. The daughter had taken up with a bad crowd that was into fast cars, alcohol, and drugs. The daughter probably was rebelling against her overly protective mother. Of acute concern was the boy she was seeing, who was the leader of the group. My friend told the parents that he would check the boy's police record and that they would then have another meeting.

He checked the FBI records and found that the boyfriend had a series of arrests for violations that were increasing in seriousness and two minor felony convictions. Then he met with the parents again and advised them of this. He also suggested that they bring their daughter in for a four-way meeting, at which he would apprise her of her boyfriend's real nature.

The four of them met soon after that, and my friend explained to the girl what he had learned about her boyfriend. She tried to act as if she already knew, but he could see that she had not known the facts. Then she cried a little, and he told her it wasn't any big deal, that he had done plenty of bad things in his life for which he could have been jailed had he been caught. She smiled and the mother squirmed.

The mother started to speak, and my friend told her to be quiet. Then he suggested to the girl that she ought to consider breaking off the relationship. "I know," she said after a long pause. The mother then said, "You can call him tonight and do it." The girl started withdrawing and my friend stepped in again. "No, she should do it face to face, if she wants to." The mother didn't like that one bit. Before she could figure out what to say next, he started discussing with the girl how and when she could meet with her boyfriend. They agreed on this, and he ended the meeting with a verbal warning to the mother to let her daughter handle it in her own way.

Later, the father called my friend to say that his daughter had lived up to her agreement with him and that he had "really used some interesting psychology" to resolve the problem. Not really—he was impartial and could see both sides, while the parents and daughter could only see their sides. That's not the point of this example, though. Rather, it's that the father saw a distress zone ahead and decided to try to do something to prevent it. And it worked. There's no telling what grief and expense that family might otherwise have experienced.

SUMMATION

I know you have probably heard that lawyers are expensive and troublesome. Unfortunately, they sometimes are—especially if you wait too long to go see one. Now let's look at the right type of lawyer.

6

Advocates

WEBSTER'S DICTIONARY defines an advocate as follows: "One who pleads another's cause, as a lawyer; one who speaks or writes in support of something." Like Webster, many lawyers consider the words "advocate" and "lawyer" to be synonymous.

Advocates come in two varieties: The first is akin to a "knight in shining armor"—someone to do battle for you against another; the second is someone to advise or counsel you—argue with you, if necessary—with regard to what legal or practical course of action you should take. The knight-in-shining-armor advocate is usually found in lawsuits or negotiating situations, such as negotiating to buy a home. The adviser advocate is usually found in nonadversary areas, such as writing a will and deciding who will get what, if you should use a trust or leave everything outright to your heirs (and risk it being squandered), and so forth. Let's look at examples of each.

THE KNIGHT IN SHINING ARMOR

Several years ago, I tried a very nasty divorce case representing the wife. The husband was about the sorriest person I'd ever encountered. He moved out on their eighteenth wedding anniversary, leaving her destitute with three teenagers. His support payments were totally inadequate, although he lavished money on his children when they came to visit him and his new girlfriend and her children. His plan was to try to cause his children to prefer to live with him, which would eliminate the support payments the court would otherwise order him to pay my client.

There were several hearings and, by the time the child custody part was heard, the husband was on his second lawyer, the first having been fired for not being mean enough. The second lawyer had been paid nothing when the child custody hearing occurred. Yet he fought like a tiger for his client, even as I smeared him in every way possible before the judge. After it was over, the judge ruled for my client on every issue and ordered the husband to pay my client's legal fees (which is customary in this type of case). I collected my fee by garnisheeing the ex-husband's wages; he never paid his lawyers, claiming poverty.

Later, the ex-husband ceased making support payments and we took him back to court about it. He had the second lawyer again, still unpaid from the previous hearing. Once again, the lawyer strongly argued his client's patently indefensible position, and again we won on all issues.

Let me explain something. The ex-husband's lawyer was an advocate. Period. You may think he was an idiot, doing all that work for nothing, and not a typical lawyer, either. Indeed, he was not typical. But he wasn't an idiot either. He undertook to represent his client after agreeing on a fee and its payment. In midstream, the bad fee bargain became obvious, but the lawyer refused to abandon his client, despicable as he was.

That lawyer was a real lawyer, one of the old school, where the duty to the client is paramount, even over the lawyer's personal or financial interests. And this is the type of knight in shining armor you will want to find, if you ever need one.

Believe it or not, there are lawyers like that one around, and they can be found and engaged. I will explain how to do this in Chapter 7, but next, let's look at an example of an adviser advocate.

ADVISERS

A young man wishing to buy a business was referred to me by an accountant. The seller had a business lawyer representing him, and it soon became obvious that I was going to be chewed up by this other lawyer, for I knew little about buying a business at that time. I referred my client to a tax lawyer friend who knew the ropes of buying a business.

My friend spent a lot of time with my client, examining the books of the new business and so forth. He concluded that my client was not mature enough nor willing to spend sufficient time to operate the business (the young man was from a wealthy family and his father was putting up the down payment). My lawyer friend also determined that the value of the business was grossly overstated—in fact, it had no real value based on present performance.

The three of us met. Without the slightest hesitation, my friend told our client the various reasons why he should not proceed. In doing so, my friend risked losing the healthy legal fee that he would earn for handling the transaction. But the client said he was determined to proceed, and my lawyer friend said, "Suit yourself, but you'll regret it." And he did. He paid my lawyer friend a large fee, bought the business, and promptly went belly-up.

SWITCHING ROLES

Often the knight-in-shining-armor advocate must also be an adviser advocate. And vice versa. Take the two examples just given.

In the divorce case, my client insisted that I make a low offer on the support issue. I felt that her offer was much too low and urged her to hold out for more, but she wouldn't change her mind. Fortunately for her, the deadbeat husband, not wanting to pay anything, declined the offer and refused to even negotiate. All the while, his lawyer was telling him he was crazy. The judge eventually awarded much more than my destitute client, who was especially anxious to settle the support issue just to get some cash flow, originally offered. Note that both lawyers laid down their armor to butt heads with their clients.

Now, look at the young man who bought the business. After he decided to proceed, several issues came up during the negotiations, one of which was how much of the value of the business would be allocated to goodwill (business reputation). That was important to my client, from a tax standpoint, because goodwill could not be depreciated (deducted from income), as could the cost of the business equipment he would be purchasing. On the other hand, the sale of the goodwill would be a favorably taxed capital gain to the seller, whereas the sale of the seller's already depreciated equipment would be taxed as an ordinary income to the seller at a much higher rate. So my client wanted to put as much of the price as possible into equipment and the seller, of course, wanted to allocate all of the price to goodwill.

My tax lawyer friend, who had been acting as adviser, took the seller's lawyer aside. Out of our client's hearing, my friend told the other lawyer that the business was clearly overpriced and that, unless the seller agreed to allocate most of the purchase price to the business equipment, there would be no deal. The seller's lawyer, not knowing that our client would have closed regardless of the allocation between equipment and goodwill, advised his client to agree to our allocation, which the seller did. This bit of *advocacy* by my lawyer friend saved our client a lot of money, even though the business eventually went broke. My young client at least was able to deduct the money he put into the deal as an ordinary loss instead of taking a long-term capital loss ("about as useful as a third ear," as tax lawyers say) on goodwill.

HIGH-POWERED ADVOCATES

The advocates described up to now are what might be described as "routine" advocates, that is to say, lawyers who routinely place a client's interests ahead of their own. Sometimes, you may need more than that in a lawyer. The following four examples demonstrate what a "high-powered" advocate can do for you—win.

In the first case, a very respected plaintiff's lawyer was representing the estate of a deceased man who had been killed in a train wreck. The facts were unfavorable: The man had driven his car into the middle of a moving train at a railroad crossing that he had crossed every day for years on his way to work. The lawyer's theory was this: There had been several lesser accidents at the crossing, and while the railroad company knew of them, it had never put up a flashing signal or other warning device. The railroad's failure to do that, the lawyer argued, negated the decedent's own carelessness (negligence, as lawyers say)

Just prior to trial, the judge called all the lawyers together to discuss settlement. He advised the plaintiff's lawyer that the plaintiff's case was very weak and that the plaintiff would do well to settle it. The judge then asked the defendant's lawyer if his client would make a settlement offer. The defense lawyer replied that an offer of $15,000 had already been made. The judge told the plaintiff's lawyer that $15,000 was a very generous offer under the facts of the case and that he should tell his client to take it. As you might imagine, that pleased the defense lawyer very much.

However, the plaintiff's lawyer replied that he felt the case was worth $75,000, and not a penny less. The judge told him that he was, in so many words, crazy—that he had seen many cases like this where the plaintiff got nothing. The plaintiff's lawyer said that he respected the judge's opinion but that he made his living representing plaintiffs, and because of that, he could evaluate a case better than a judge any day of the week. The lawyer then repeated his demand for $75,000, and said that if the defendant did not pay it, the case would be tried. Fearing the ability of the plaintiff's lawyer, the defendant raised the offer to $50,000 and the case was settled, much to the consternation of the defense lawyer and the judge.

In another case, a man tried to sell his home. Before putting it on the market, he contacted his lender about a buyer assuming (taking over) the loan on the home. The lender told him that it could not be assumed under any circumstances. The man had papers given to him at the closing saying that the loan could be assumed at prevailing interest rates, if the new buyer's credit checked out. The man pointed that out to the lender to no avail. The loan had been sold by the lender to the Federal National Mortgage Association (commonly known as "Fanny Mae"), which had a policy of not allowing any of its loans to be assumed. So the man forgot about the assumption idea and unsuccessfully tried for months to sell his home to a buyer who could refinance.

The next thing to happen was that the man learned he was being transferred to another state, which meant he would have to leave his unsold home vacant—a terrible thing to do. Not only would that reduce its marketability, it would invite vandalism and cause him to lose his property insurance. So, he came to me, knowing I handled a lot of residential real estate matters.

After a little investigation, I learned the following juicy facts: My client's original lender had signed a "buy back and hold harmless agreement" with Fanny Mae. In essence, if my client were to sue Fanny Mae over its assumption policy, then Fanny Mae could require the original lender to defend the lawsuit, buy back the loan, and pay any damages my client might be awarded. Because of that agreement, which is standard with all Fanny Mae loans, Fanny Mae felt that it was in a position to deny the assumption of its loans with impunity.

I threatened to sue Fanny Mae for violation of the federal truth-in-lending laws and outrageous conduct. I quickly got a telephone call from the original lender giving us the go-ahead for an assumption sale. I said it was too late—that my client had been severely injured and would sue for damages.

All along, I knew that the original lender would not let me sue Fanny Mae, which bought most of the loans it originated, because if the original lender lost Fanny Mae's favor, thus its business, it would be hurt badly. In the end, the original lender bought my client's home for cash at a price higher than what he could have obtained from a buyer assuming his loan. The lender also paid my fee, leaving me with a very happy client.

In a third case, a man was charged with statutory rape, meaning that he had sexual intercourse with a willing female under the legal age of consent. The man was a high school teacher and the "victim" was one of his students. The victim's outraged parents instituted the criminal proceeding and, as a result, the man lost his job and was forced into bankruptcy.

In a case like this, there is no *legal* defense. The man did it, the girl was under age, so the man was guilty. The defense lawyer knew that the only way to win was to pick a jury that would be sympathetic to the man's plight, or at least unsympathetic to the victim. So the lawyer hired a psychologist to help him pick the jury.

The jury panel ended up consisting of men and women who had little regard for the legal process or law enforcement. To them, a case such as this one was simply a "tempest in a teapot." They also felt that the defendant had suffered enough, especially in view of the fact that the victim, also a party to the "crime," was getting off scot-free. So they acquitted the man.

In the fourth case, a woman was severely burned when her Ford Pinto exploded when struck from the rear. After a lot of digging, the plaintiff's lawyer representing the woman located someone in Ford Motor Company willing to talk and furnish evidence. Here's what the lawyer found out.

Ford had known of the tendency of Pintos to explode on rear-end impact. In fact, there were movies made by Ford technicians of Pintos exploding in field tests. Ford's management had weighed the cost of a major recall against the potential legal costs and damages that would arise out of Pinto lawsuits. It appeared that the recall cost would outweigh the legal costs and damages by about $150 million. Ford's management decided not to recall the Pintos.

When this shocking evidence was presented to the jury, it returned a verdict of almost $150 million—about what Ford had calculated it would save by not recalling the Pinto.

SUMMATION

You should now have a better understanding of what an advocate is and how one behaves. You definitely will want this type of lawyer—even if he hurts your feelings when he advises you. Now let's look at how to pick a lawyer.

7

Selecting the Right Lawyer

IN THIS CHAPTER, I will share with you what I know about selecting a lawyer and winning the lottery. There's no guarantee that these methods will work *every* time. However, I believe that your chances of picking a good lawyer will be greatly improved, if you try to use what follows.

The first order of business is to know what lawyers to avoid.

LAWYERS TO AVOID

Shysters. Avoid all shysters (described in Chapter 2). You will recognize some shysters immediately. Others, you may not recognize until after you have met with them. In any event, as soon as you realize that you are dealing with one, consider terminating the relationship (explained in Chapter 14).

Conflict of Interest. Avoid any lawyer who has a conflict of interest (explained in Chapter 3) between you and someone else involved in your case. Often a lawyer will say, "I have a *potential* conflict of interest, but feel I can handle the case at this point. If the conflict becomes *real*, I will let you know." If you fall for that line, you risk at the very least having to find another lawyer in midstream. At the worst, you risk not learning of the conflict until after you have been damaged by it. Think about conflict of interest as being similar to the topic in this famous saying: "You can't be just a little bit pregnant."

Friends and Relatives. Don't use one. First, you probably will expect a reduced, or perhaps no, fee. That tends to make any lawyer less interested in your case. Second, you will carry the baggage of your present relationship into the lawyer-client relationship, which will affect the lawyer's ability to be impartial.

For instance, if the lawyer is overly sensitive to you, it will be tough for him to say what's really on his mind, especially if he knows you don't want to hear it. If you are the sensitive one, you may react too emotionally to candid advice or suggestions and not really hear what is being said. Or, what if the lawyer fouls up the case? Will you be able to fire him, initiate a grievance against him, or sue him for malpractice? Regardless, things will never be the same when you see each other at parties or over Thanksgiving dinner.

"Practicing" Lawyers. As a general rule, you should use a seasoned (experienced) lawyer. That means you should stay away, if at all possible, from new lawyers or those who don't normally handle the type of case that you have. As I pointed out earlier, lawyers, unlike doctors, are not required to serve an internship or do a residency under the supervision of other lawyers. All that a lawyer needs to do legal work is a law license. After he has it, he can then start "practicing" on you!

Lawyers Who Aren't Busy. If a lawyer is not busy, that's a sign that he's either a new lawyer or hasn't impressed his clients with his abilities. Rather, he's impressed them with his lack thereof. Go somewhere else.

Lawyers Who Are too Busy. These are very good lawyers, so good in fact that they have more business than they can handle. The result is that your case is handled by another lawyer in the firm, or the one you want takes forever to do it. I know many fine lawyers like this— ones I wouldn't hesitate to use myself, but for the delays I would experience.

Stone-Age Lawyers. Those who don't use computers. If the lawyer doesn't have a computer—or an advanced word processor—document preparation will be grueling and expensive. If your case involves a lawsuit, your lawyer will be like the Polish horse cavalry charging a German Panzer tank—he'll be mowed down. If the lawyer is writing a complex legal document such as a business agreement or a will with trust provisions, it will take him forever to do it, and you will pay for the extra time it takes him to do the work.

Lawyers with Personal Problems. It probably would be wise to avoid a lawyer going through a divorce, child custody fight, bankruptcy, criminal prosecution, illness, or the like, or one who is defending a serious grievance complaint or any type of malpractice suit. Even the best lawyer will be distracted by that kind of thing, and you could suffer for it. I know you are wondering how you learn about these things. The answer is very simple: Ask the lawyer. But be sure to explain why you want to know. If the lawyer's a good one, he will be impressed by your concern and will tell you. If he's not, he will start acting weird or may even refuse to answer you. If that happens, be nice, conclude the interview, and look for another lawyer.

Now that you know what lawyers to avoid, the question is whom do you pick. Thus your next decision is whether to use a "general practitioner" (G.P.) or a "specialist."

GENERAL PRACTITIONERS VS. SPECIALISTS

Many general practitioners handle a variety of cases very well. It usually takes them a little longer to do so than it would a specialist (and it may cost more), and sometimes they don't get quite the results that a specialist would. The reason is that the specialist stays on top of one area and knows the very latest legal developments and methods. On the other hand, your case may involve other legal matters about which the specialist may know little or nothing. Therefore, while the specialist is doing you a very good job on your main problem, he may be creating another problem for you somewhere else.

It can work the other way, too. The G.P. can overlook something very important that a specialist would catch. For instance, a tax lawyer friend had a client come to him with a tax problem. In looking through the client's business records, my friend noticed that the business, a corporation, had elected Subchapter S treatment under the tax laws. Such an election allows a business to pass its losses through to the shareholders, as if there was no corporation at all. Subchapter S typically is elected by newly formed corporations that stand to lose money in the early years of the business operation.

The client's business was such a business, there being large losses in the early years. Unfortunately, the G.P. who incorporated the business allowed the client's uncle, a Greek citizen and resident, to become a stockholder. This voided the Subchapter S election, as only U.S. citizens could be stockholders. The G.P. knew the general rules and benefits of a Subchapter S, but missed a very important requirement that lost the client several thousand dollars.

Often a G.P. and a specialist will work together on a case. Say your spouse is killed in an automobile accident caused by someone else. In all likelihood, you would want a damage suit specialist to handle the claim against the person at fault. But you would want a G.P. to handle the estate work. If, however, your spouse left a large estate and there are estate tax matters to resolve, you probably will want to use an estate tax specialist instead of a G.P. for that part of the case. Two specialists, in other words.

Later in this chapter, I will explain how to locate a specialist for your case, but let me say here that you might even need a G.P. to coordinate matters between the damage suit and estate tax specialists in the above example. That, of course, would depend on the size of your spouse's estate, the potential recovery in the damage suit, and so forth. As a general rule of thumb, the more money that is involved, the more types of lawyers you will probably need.

It would be nice if the G.P. and specialist(s) both worked in the same law firm. Unfortunately, it doesn't usually work out that way. For instance, you seldom see damage suit, divorce, or criminal lawyers in firms that handle business, tax, or estate work. If your case is a big one, be prepared to deal with more than one law firm.

Related to the G.P./specialist decision is the question of whether or not to use a firm that offers reasonable fees for a limited variety of "routine" cases, instead of a G.P. or a specialist.

LEGAL CLINICS

Legal clinics are sometimes an excellent alternative to either a G.P. or a specialist. But not always. They are not good for complicated, unusual, or large cases. Here are the types of cases you go to a legal clinic for: *simple* bankruptcy or debtor's court; *uncontested* divorce (remember what I said about both of you using the same lawyer); *simple* wills; *simple* real estate closings; *small* damage suits; *simple* estates (someone has died); adoptions; changes-of-name; removing a minor's disabilities of non-age (a court order allowing a minor to be treated as an adult); foreclosing a defaulted mortgage owed to you; and defending *small* suits against you.

You might also consider using a legal clinic's lawyers to advise you on an hourly basis, when you think that you might be falling into a distress zone (see Chapter 5). And a legal clinic is a good place to go to learn who the specialists are in your locality.

This brings us to the point of choosing the right lawyer for you.

CHOOSING THE LAWYER

It has been pointed out that only a few state bar associations or commissions recognize or certify law specialties (such as tort litigation, real estate, divorce, criminal law, and taxation). Therefore, picking the right lawyer, whether a G.P., a specialist, or a legal clinic, can be very difficult in most states. Here are some ways to improve the odds.

Lawyer-Brokers. My first suggestion is to let another lawyer suggest two or three other lawyers for you to interview. As I mentioned above, using a legal clinic for this is often a good idea. Or you might use a lawyer you already know. I like the idea of using a lawyer to pick your lawyer, because a lawyer is the person who is most likely to know who is the best lawyer for your case and whether or not you and he are well suited, personalitywise. In other words, use the selecting lawyer as an impartial observer/adviser—a lawyer-broker, so to speak. I would consider paying for this service by the hour. Or, you can use the lawyer-broker fee arrangement suggested in the next chapter. But be sure and read that chapter *before* attempting to use a lawyer as a lawyer-broker in a case that would get the lawyer a referral fee from a specialist.

If you decide to use a lawyer as a lawyer-broker, be on guard for the following: He may suggest himself as being the type of lawyer you need, or he may try to make an outrageous referral fee for doing nothing. Don't let him handle the case or rip you off on the referral. One other thing. Try to find out if your lawyer-broker sends a lot of business to the other lawyer, and vice versa. If so, the referral may be more in the referring lawyer's best interest than in yours. That's why you want to get two or three names. Then interview each lawyer recommended.

Lawyer Referral Services. Be careful here. Most local bar associations offer a lawyer's referral service. You can call it and get referred to a "specialist." Be advised that most referral services do not check out the credentials of a participating lawyer. In other words, any such lawyer could have his name listed as handling divorces, corporations, patent law, or whatever, without ever having handled that type of case. Lawyers who offer to accept referrals from referral services usually either are new lawyers or are not busy enough. Both types are the kind you should try to avoid. However, if you don't know a lawyer, you may consider using a referral service to put you in touch with a lawyer, who can then act as a lawyer-broker for you.

Friends or Relatives. If you have friends or relatives who have had good dealings with a lawyer, go see that lawyer. If it turns out that the lawyer does not handle your type of case, he still might make an excellent lawyer-broker.

Accountants, Bank Officers, Insurance People. These people deal with lawyers all the time and usually will know a lawyer who handles your kind of case. A word of warning. You may be referred to one of their friends or relatives or someone who sends them business, meaning you shouldn't blindly accept the referral. Use the suggestions made in this chapter to check out whomever they recommend.

Court Clerks. They know who handles what type of cases and whether or not they do it well. If you are faced, say, with a divorce, go to the divorce court clerk and ask the names of the three lawyers who do the most divorce work.

Judges. What was said about court clerks also applies to judges.

Your Minister. A minister spends a lot of time trying to help people work out their problems. Often, he refers parishioners to lawyers. Since the minister gets nothing in return for the referral, it will not be tainted. Also, the minister hears from his parishioners about how the lawyer treated them and how the case came out. Therefore, he is not likely to refer you to an abusive or an incompetent lawyer.

Now you are ready to meet with a lawyer, so let's look at the first meeting.

THE INITIAL INTERVIEW

When you decide on a lawyer to interview, call to make an appointment with the following in mind. You will be the *employer*, he the potential *employee*. If you decide to hire him, the lawyer will work on a matter that is important to *you*. Therefore, you will want to size him up, face to face—just like anyone else you would hire to work for you, glowing references notwithstanding. Accordingly, the purpose of the initial meeting will not be to get legal advice. Rather, it will be to decide if you want to use the lawyer at all.

Making the Appointment. You should speak to the lawyer, not his secretary, when you call for an appointment. Explain to him that you need to hire a lawyer, say, for a divorce or to have a will prepared, and that you would like to arrange a get-acquainted—not a working—meeting. Ask him if he will do this for no charge, because you will not be asking for legal advice at the meeting. Some lawyers do not like to do that, because they often end up giving free advice at first meetings arranged on that basis. A lawyer who does not offer a free get-acquainted interview is not to be automatically rejected, for he may still be the best lawyer for you and your case. However, if you use the approach suggested, your odds of getting a free interview will be enhanced. They will be further enhanced if the lawyer stands to make a good fee.

How Long an Interview? For most cases, one hour should be enough time to outline your case to and size up the lawyer. Any longer than that will get you into talking about the specifics of your case and cause the lawyer to start thinking, "I've been had again." That's not a good way to start the relationship.

Sleuth Work. What you are looking for at the get-acquainted meeting are subjective signs or clues about the lawyer—his "breeding," if you will—as well as hard facts. For instance: Is he polite? Does he look you in the eye when he talks, or does he look out the window? Does he dress neatly? Are his eyes clear, or do they look like road maps? Is he a slob, either in appearance or in the way he keeps his office? If so, he will keep your case that way, too. Is he having his telephone calls held while you are there? If not, he's not concentrating on you, nor is he very polite. Is he a good listener and patient, or does he do most of the talking? Do the two of you seem to be compatible? If you feel uncomfortable about the lawyer in any of these areas, it's not a good sign.

Look around his offices. Do you see a computer/word processor anywhere? Does he have a law library? If so, are the supplements in the backs of the law books this year's? If not, he's not current on the law, and he may be having a cash flow problem that prevents him from buying the supplements. If he does not have a law library, ask him where he does research. Consider also the decor of his offices. Are they tastefully done, or are they run down or perhaps too lavish? If they are run down, the lawyer may be on hard times financially. If lavish, you may be gouged on the fee to help pay for it.

Questions to Ask. Earlier in this chapter, I suggested some questions that you should ask your lawyer, i.e., is he in bankruptcy, facing a divorce, etc.? The get-acquainted meeting is the time to ask those questions—politely. Apologize for having to ask them, but do it anyway. Also, ask the lawyer if he or another lawyer in the firm will handle your case. If it will be another lawyer, you should have a similar meeting (at another time) with that lawyer, before making a decision. This is also the time to find out if there is a conflict of interest problem. Tell the lawyer the names of all involved and ask if he represents or ever has represented any of them. If so, conclude the interview and look for another lawyer.

That behind you, it's time to question the lawyer about his practice. If you are there, say, to have a will written, ask him how many wills he writes a year. If your will requirements are complex, requiring trusts, ask him how many complex wills or trusts he does a year. If it's for a divorce or to defend a damage suit (or to prosecute one), ask the same types of questions. If he says something like "a lot," "I know how to do that," or "let me tell you about the last one of those that I did," look out. What you are after here is *frequency*, not generalities or one success story.

Other Clients. Also ask the lawyer if he can give you the names of a few clients for whom he has done similar work. He can't divulge this without their permission, but if he's good, he will have several clients who will be willing to talk with you. If he won't cooperate with you here, then I would tend to be suspicious of his ability, but I would not cross him off my list just yet. Here's why. Many lawyers just aren't used to being "interviewed"—especially about their own clients—so a negative reaction may not necessarily be a bad sign.

Malpractice Insurance. You definitely want your lawyer to have this, because if he fouls up your case, his insurance will pay for your loss. If you are dealing with an established, prosperous lawyer, you probably won't have to risk insulting him by asking to see a copy of his policy. However, if you are dealing with a new or questionable lawyer, you shouldn't do anything until you see it. The reason is 20 to 25 percent of all lawyers do not carry malpractice insurance!

The Fee in General. If things have gone well up to now, ask the lawyer about the fees he charges for your type of case. Negotiating fees is discussed in depth in Chapter 8. This meeting may not be the best time to do that, for what you are after now is a general feel for the lawyer—not a business deal. That, perhaps, should occur in another meeting, assuming you decide he is a good lawyer for you and your case.

Shop Around. Interview some more lawyers—two or three perhaps. Use the same techniques. Narrow down your choice, then discuss the fee. Then make your decision and hire the lawyer you have chosen. Remember, the lawyer will cost you somewhere between the price of a small television (for a will) and that of a car (for a lawsuit). You shop around for those, don't you?

The Employment Agreement. Once you and your lawyer shake hands on the deal, ask him to write you a letter explaining what he is to do for you and how much it is going to cost. The letter should outline in plain English what to expect, about how long it will take, and who will be handling the work. The letter should also state that you will be receiving copies of all court papers, letters, documents, and so forth that pertain to your case. That will keep you up to date and minimize the possibility of a lack-of-communication problem. Do not give the lawyer any money or let him do any work on your case until you have this letter.

SUMMATION

Few clients select the right lawyer for them or their case. Getting along with the lawyer is just as important as the lawyer's ability or availability. Even fewer clients understand that it's their case, not the lawyer's, and that they, not the lawyer, are the boss. Those facts are, in my judgment, why many people feel that they have had bad dealings with lawyers. Lack of communication is another problem area. The final and probably the biggest gripe people have about lawyers, the fee, is examined in the next chapter.

Let me leave you with this last thought about interviewing a lawyer. Do not go in waving this book in his face, saying Bashinsky suggested this or that. In fact, don't do anything that would come across as your being a smart aleck or know-it-all—even if you do know it all, which isn't likely. A lawyer-client relationship is like a marriage. The interview is the courtship. So be polite and businesslike.

Now, let's look at the numbers.

8

The Lawyer's Fee

I HAVE MENTIONED THAT when I was in law school one of my professors was a man named Sam Beatty. For years, he had been called "Bad Sam," a name he had earned by habitually giving about half his students D's or F's. His reputation struck fear into every new student's heart. I met Bad Sam the second semester of my freshman year. I was the first student he called on. I'll never forget it. "Bashiiiinsky," he said with a leering grin, "I like that name, Bashiiinsky." I was probably the first law student of Polish extraction to come before him. As soon as he called my name, I dutifully stood up to receive his question, as was the custom.

"Mr. Bashinsky, what's the first thing you do when a client comes into your office?" he asked with a twinkle in his eye.

I knew I was in big trouble, because the question had nothing to do with the homework assignment for that day. But, being a hopeful soul, I said, "Ask him why he came to see me?"

Bad Sam's mocking words, "Sit down, Bashinsky. You'll never make it as a lawyer," never left me. Nor did the correct answer, which he elicited after several of my fellow students were similarly put down.

"YOU GET PAID!!!"

That was my introduction to Bad Sam's impromptu courses in practical law. Later, in actual practice, I learned how correct he was. In general, people just don't like paying for a lawyer's services. And I quickly found that, if I didn't get paid up front in certain types of cases, I never got paid at all. The knight-in-shining-armor advocate in Chapter 6 apparently had not taken any courses under Bad Sam.

I developed a unique approach for collecting at least part of my fee up front from clients who wanted to string me along until the end. It goes something like this:

Me: "You know, I'm just like you?"

Client: "Yeah, how so?"

Me: "I can only think about one thing at a time."

Client: "What do you mean?"

Me: "Well, as long as I'm worried about getting paid for all of the work I'm going to do for you, I will have a tough time worrying about solving your problem!"

Client: "Oh. I see what you mean!"

Another clever remark I often make is this:

"I'm not a bank. If you want to borrow money, go to the bank. Don't borrow it from me."

That's the lawyer's point of view. The other side of the coin is expressed by the results of a recent survey of lay opinion about lawyers by *USA Today*. The far-and-away biggest complaint about lawyers found in the survey was high legal fees.

TUG-OF-WAR

The problem is this. Lawyers have to earn fees to stay in business and pay their personal financial obligations. Like anyone else, they also tend to want to make as much money as possible so that they can enjoy a high standard of living.

You, on the other hand, may be faced with a legal problem you don't even want—one that could prove expensive, such as a divorce or damage suit against you, or one that could put you away in prison for a while. Then, on top of that, you have to shell out a lot of money for a lawyer to handle your uninvited problem. Let's just say you're not overjoyed about all of this. Or, you just need a "simple" will drawn, but the lawyer doesn't see that what you want to accomplish with your estate plan is as simple as you think it is—that you need a trust to fully protect your children, for example—and the trust will cost an additional $500.

While the lawyer has a duty to be your advocate—protect you at just about all costs—that duty normally does not arise until you have actually hired the lawyer. And part of hiring the lawyer is reaching an agreement on the lawyer's fee. Until that issue is resolved, the lawyer is really in an adversarial or opposing position to you—a conflict of interest, if you will. Therefore, the fee must be decided upon before the lawyer can really become your advocate.

You will be very lucky to find a lawyer like the knight in shining armor described in Chapter 6—one who will work for nothing. But even in that example, the fee arrangement was decided up front, before any work was done. The lawyer simply made a mistake by agreeing to be paid later, rather than at the beginning. You will find that most lawyers will require payment up front in divorce, child custody, criminal, and similar distress zone cases. In other types of cases, the fee arrangement will be different.

Now, let's look at the different types of fees that lawyers charge.

FEE ARRANGEMENTS

By the Hour. Many types of cases lend themselves to a fee charged by the hour. Hourly rates can vary greatly, depending on such factors as your ability to pay, the complexity of the case, the amount of money involved, the lawyer's unique skill or expertise in the area, the lawyer's view of fees in general (some are more interested in lawyering than gouging clients, and vice versa), and the lawyer's financial situation (the higher his living standard, the bigger his fees will be).

Hourly fees typically range from $50 to $300 per hour, depending on the factors mentioned above. Older partners in a firm charge higher hourly fees than the younger partners or associates (lawyers who are not partners). Believe me, hourly fees are negotiable, and you can get a better rate by comparing prices and playing lawyers off against each other. If you are poor and cannot afford large legal fees, know that some lawyers will reduce their fees or do *pro bono* (free) work for poor clients whose cases are deserving.

The following are examples of hourly fee type cases: defending a damage suit, writing a will, drawing up a contract, negotiating the purchase of a home or investment property, checking title on real estate, child adoption, and preparing a tax return.

In addition to the hourly fee, you will be charged for expenses the lawyer incurs in your behalf. Such expenses will be those that pertain to your particular case, as opposed to the lawyer's general operating expenses. What we're talking about here are such things as the following: court filing fees, document recording fees, postage, copying, mileage, room and board for out-of-town travel, deposition (out of court testimony) costs, outside investigator fees, photographs, and expert witness fees. You may be asked to pay these costs as they are incurred. Those expenses can add up to a lot of money in some cases, so tell your lawyer, in writing, that you don't want him to incur any costs (other than his fee) without prior approval from you.

Many lawyers will require a retainer to be paid up front, to be applied against the fee as it is earned. For instance, if you agree to pay your lawyer $75 per hour to negotiate a real estate purchase, the lawyer may require a $500 retainer. If the lawyer works ten hours, you will owe $250 at the end (10 hours × $75 per hour less the $500 retainer). If the lawyer works only four hours, then he has earned only $300 (4 hours × $75 per hour). If the retainer is refundable, you are due a $200 refund. If not, you get nothing back. Whether or not the retainer is refundable is negotiable—but in most cases, it will be nonrefundable. You will also owe the lawyer for any costs he incurred in your behalf that you have not already paid.

Clients often balk at paying the retainer. If you are in this category, consider how that affects the lawyer, who is worried about not getting paid. Do you want to start off the relationship with your lawyer not trusting you? Furthermore, clients who have paid a retainer invariably listen better to what their lawyer has to say. As a result, they often are happier when the case is over. Thus, it usually is best to pay a reasonable retainer up front.

In addition to negotiating the hourly fee and the retainer, you should also try to get the lawyer to agree to put a cap (top limit) on what the total bill will be. Unless the case is very unusual, he should be able to size it up and make a pretty good guestimate of what he will have to do. A lawyer who won't do this probably doesn't know enough about your type of case to figure the time he has in it, or is greedy for your money. There are far too many lawyers who are more interested in running up their hourly charges than in resolving the client's problem. Especially guilty of that are defense lawyers who usually handle lawsuits on an hourly basis. Therefore, beware of lawyers who are unwilling to limit their hourly fees.

Related to the "fee generator" is the "fee inventor," the lawyer who charges you for work never done—if you let him. That type, described in the following joke, also can be held at bay by capping his fee.

> A lawyer died and was met by St. Peter at the pearly gates.
> "There must be some mistake," the lawyer complained.
> "Why is that?" asked St. Peter.
> "Because I'm only forty-two years old!" exclaimed the lawyer.
> "Oh? According to your billed hours, you are eighty-seven!"

The Flat Fee. Related to the hourly fee with a cap is the flat fee arrangement. Here, you simply agree to pay a set amount for the case. Take the real estate purchase example on page 58. Instead of charging you by the hour, the lawyer may want to charge $750 for the deal. Here's another example.

Suppose you are getting a divorce. The lawyer may agree to handle it for $2,000. If the case settles, though, the lawyer will be overpaid for the time spent. To prevent this, get the lawyer to agree to two flat fees—$1,000 if the case settles, $2,000 if it is tried. As with the hourly fee arrangement, the lawyer may want part of the flat fee paid up front as a retainer. The expenses will be paid by you in one of the ways suggested above.

I tend to prefer the hourly fee with a cap to the flat fee. Here's why. It leaves the door open for you to get out for less, if the case doesn't take as long as planned. For instance, if the real estate deal mentioned above only takes eight hours of the lawyer's time, then he's earned $600 (8 hours × $75 per hour), and you've saved $150 ($750 less $600). Or, in the divorce example, if the lawyer tries the case to conclusion but has only spent twenty hours on it, he's earned $1,500 (20 hours × $75 per hour), saving you $500 ($2,000 less $1,500). Also, the flat fee doesn't flush out the greedy or inexperienced lawyer the way an hourly fee with a cap does.

Up-front Fees. I suggested that lawyers like to get paid everything up front in certain types of cases, typically divorce, child custody, and criminal cases. The reason is that if they don't do this, they often don't get paid. That's their side of it. Now here's your side.

Often, once the lawyer has the whole fee, he gets lazy. He's eaten the carrot, and you now have only a bare stick to wave in front of his nose. Take this case. A firm I know handled an income tax evasion matter and charged their client $70,000 up front for the whole case. It got a lot more involved than they had anticipated, and after giving him $70,000 of their time, they turned their attention to more rewarding cases. This could have been avoided perhaps by putting half, or $35,000, of the fee in escrow with a bank or another law firm (or with a lawyer-broker), to be paid on conclusion of the case.

Monthly Retainer. If you are a regular client of the lawyer, he may try to put you on what is called a "monthly retainer." Here you pay a fixed sum per month, say $500, for the privilege of being able to call on the lawyer for routine advice and minor work. I do not like this arrangement from either the client's or lawyer's side. Clients invariably feel they aren't getting their money's worth, and lawyers, of course, feel that they are doing more work than they are getting paid to do. Large corporations often keep a law firm on retainer; however,

I do not feel that an individual should do it. Just pay the lawyer as you use him. You will get along better.

Contingency Fees. Contingency fees are used when the client wants the lawyer to share the risk of recovering something from somebody. For instance, damages for injuries received in an automobile accident, money you loaned to someone that hasn't been repaid, or real estate that you and someone else both claim to own. In those cases, the lawyer gets a percentage of whatever is recovered—if it's recovered. If no recovery is made, the lawyer, like you, gets nothing. So, this arrangement causes the lawyer to work very hard.

Sometimes a contingency fee is used when a client is being audited by the IRS. For example, if the IRS claims that you owe an extra $10,000 in back taxes, the lawyer may agree to defend the claim for a percentage of what he saves you, often 50 percent. A word to the wise. To a tax lawyer, this type of case usually is like shooting fish in a barrel. He knows that the revenue agent will make concessions to get some money paid and the file closed. So, keep the percentage on the low side.

Another example would be if you are injured in an automobile accident and are not at fault. The other side's insurance company offers to pay your medical bills, repair your car, furnish you a rental car to drive, and pay you $5,000 for your pain and suffering. Before accepting such an offer, let a good plaintiff's attorney evaluate it. He may tell you that $5,000 is a reasonable offer, or he may feel that you are being ripped off and that you should get $50,000 in view of your injuries.

If you decide to let him try for more than has been offered, get him to agree that his percentage fee will be computed only against what he can obtain over and above what you were already offered. Suppose that your medical bills are $7,200, car repairs are $3,200, and the rental car cost is $600, or a total cost to you of $11,000. And suppose further that your lawyer recovers $50,000. If his fee is one-third of the recovery, he gets $13,000 ([$50,000 less $11,000] × .333). You get the rest. In this example, the lawyer's true percentage fee is thus 26 percent ($13,000 divided by $50,000 × 100 percent).

Typically, a percentage arrangement will run from 10 to 50 percent of the recovery (or savings), depending on the facts of your case. This amount is negotiable, and you can get a better deal by shopping around. For instance, if the lawyer you really want to use says 40 percent is as low as he will go, and you know Lawyer Able down the street will do it for 35 percent, say so. That might get the lawyer to come down. If you do this, it would be a good idea to really have gotten a 35 percent quote from Lawyer Able, just in case he and your lawyer play golf or racquetball together. Otherwise, you could end up with a disgruntled lawyer—not a good thing to have.

Another consideration is having the contingency fee work on a sliding scale. For example, the lawyer might agree to take only 10 percent if the case is settled before suit is filed, 25 percent if it is settled after suit is filed, and 40 percent if the case is tried. Under this arrangement, he is paid more for doing more work. Under a straight contingency, he is paid the same percentage regardless of how hard he works.

Depending on your case and, perhaps, the lawyer's financial condition, he may want you to guarantee the expenses—if the case is lost—or even pay them as they are incurred. Try to avoid that arrangement. When the lawyer is working on a contingency basis (no win, no pay) and is footing the expenses, he will work a lot harder than he would if you were paying the expenses—especially if they will be large. Also, if the lawyer can't afford to eat the expenses if the case is lost, it probably means either that he's having financial problems or doesn't handle enough good contingency cases to finance the new ones coming in. A bad sign, in other words.

Some lawyers will tell you it's illegal not to charge you for the expenses if you lose a contingency case, because that constitutes "maintenance." That ancient English law term describes a lawyer who finances lawsuits that otherwise would not be brought. The lawyer will be telling you the truth, because it is illegal. However, damage suit lawyers routinely disregard this rule, and you should be able to convince yours to do the same or find another lawyer who will. Any lawyer who quotes this rule to you is either weak financially or too inexperienced to risk the expenses.

Now, I'm not saying *never* use a lawyer who charges you for expenses, win or lose, in a contingency case. There are a few situations where it would be appropriate. For instance, the prospect of winning may be marginal, but the case is important to you. For your sake, the lawyer may be willing to risk his time but not the expenses to help you out. Or, perhaps the case is too small or unusual to interest the good lawyers. But you have found an eager, young lawyer with plenty of time on his hands, who is willing to give it a shot if you pay the expenses.

One final thing about contingency fees that I have seen cause a lot of problems. Obviously, it's a no-win, no-pay situation for your lawyer. Unless he's well-heeled, a good settlement offer from the other side will sorely tempt him to talk you into taking the offer and "running like a thief," as the judge advised Galvin in the movie *The Verdict* (see Appendix). A damage suit specialist with the wolf at the door is going to cause you problems here. So stay on your toes, if that's the type of lawyer you have.

Attorney's Fees by Agreement. In breach of contract cases, there often is a provision in the contract allowing the side not in breach (or the winner of a lawsuit filed to enforce the contract) to recover legal fees from the other side. In such cases, the amount of the fee is usually set by the court at an amount that the court feels is reasonable for the case. But you would be lucky to get the lawyer to agree to accept only what the other side is required to pay. First, if the case is settled out of court, the fee may never be determined. Second, the fee awarded is usually less than the lawyer is willing to take. If you are working with a lawyer, he probably will want to set his own fee, then apply whatever the court awards against the fee that he has earned.

Let's look at an example. If Smith owes you $2,500 for remodeling his den and your contract has an attorney fee provision, the court will give you a $2,500 judgment against Smith, plus an attorney fee of, say, $500. If your lawyer wants one-third of the recovery, then his fee either will be $833 (1/3 × $2,500), or, if you aren't careful, $1,000 (1/3 × $3,000). In other words, be sure to apply the lawyer's percentage to what will be awarded you *before* attorney's fees. Then use the attorney's fee award, when collected, to help pay the lawyer.

Court-awarded Fees. In some cases, especially divorce and child custody cases, the court will award an attorney's fee to a spouse (or parent), if he or she does not have funds to pay a lawyer. For instance, if you are a housewife and have no earnings, the court will set a fee and require your husband (or ex-husband) to pay it. Divorce lawyers often take cases on this basis alone. At other times, they ask for a retainer up front and agree to get the rest of their fee from the other side. Sometimes, they will require you to pay the entire fee but will give you credit for what the court requires the other side to pay. Knowing these options will enable you to shop around and get a better deal on the fee. If expenses have been incurred by the lawyer handling your case, the court may order the other side to pay them as well. But your lawyer might want you to foot the bill in the meantime.

The court awards fees in some uncontested types of cases, too, such as handling an estate. A formula is often used that turns out to be quite favorable to your lawyer. Of course, it looks perfectly okay to you because the judge, not your lawyer, sets the fee. Reread Chapter 4 on the lawyer brotherhood, and then you will view the fee set by that nice, old judge a little differently.

By the way, you don't have to let this happen. Instead, get the lawyer to agree to handle the estate, say, by the hour with a cap. Be prepared to shop the case to other lawyers, too. If the lawyer agrees to the fee, then the court won't become involved in that part of your case. Use this method any time the lawyer says, "We'll let the court set my fee."

By Statute. In special cases, an act of Congress or of your state legislature provides for the recovery of attorney's fees. The amount is set either in the statute or by the court and may or may not be satisfactory to your lawyer. Here, though, the lawyer's feelings are often irrelevant; for the statute might specifically provide that the statutory or court-awarded fee is all that the lawyer can collect—a point that you should discuss with your lawyer. In fact, ask for a copy of that portion of the statute pertaining to attorney's fees. That way, you will be sure.

Examples of the types of cases when attorney's fees are awarded under a statute are worker's compensation; social security and other government welfare benefits; sex, race, and age discrimination; securities violations; antitrust violations; frivolous lawsuits filed against you; harassment or bad faith by the IRS or other government agencies; denial of access under the Freedom of Information Act, and so forth. *Public Citizen* magazine, founded by Ralph Nader, or HALT (Americans for Legal Reform), both located in Washington, D.C., can advise you more thoroughly in this area.

As to expenses, the statutes also provide for these, too. Again, get a copy of the law that governs your case from your lawyer and read it before agreeing to anything.

Bankruptcy and Debtor's Court. Your attorney's fee is set (or approved) by the court and is paid out of your funds, if any. In a straight bankruptcy—where you go completely belly-up—your lawyer will want to be paid up front, and will worry later about getting the court to approve the fee. Otherwise, he may have to share the "slim pickin's" with your other creditors. In a debtor's court case, where you consolidate your debts and get better payment terms, the lawyer will get paid ahead of your creditors out of your monthly payments into the court, so you should not have to pay your lawyer a fee up front. In a "reorganization" case, which is like a business "debtor's court," your lawyer will want to be paid up front, as in a straight bankruptcy case. In any bankruptcy case, you will have to pay the filing fee, which is not large, in advance.

Indigent Legal Services. Poor people often can obtain representation at no charge through state or U.S. government programs. The more common ones use the public defender or court-appointed programs (criminal cases) or the Legal Services Corporation (nonfee-generating civil cases). The lawyers in those programs are usually dedicated to their work, but often are overworked and fresh out of law school. Call your local bar association to find out what programs like these are offered where you live.

The foregoing covers, generally, the different types of fee arrangements and offers suggestions to minimize the amount you will have to pay. If you are being referred by one lawyer to another, you should consider the following.

REFERRAL FEES

I've explained that lawyers who refer cases to other lawyers often get a referral fee for doing so. That usually happens in a contingency fee type of case, such as a damage suit. Recalling the example in Chapter 4 of the lawyer who referred a damage suit to a specialist, the specialist settled the case for $400,000, kept $100,000, gave the clients $200,000, then sent the remaining $100,000 as a referral fee to the first lawyer.

I'm sure you're thinking that by going directly to the specialist, the client could have saved $100,000. Perhaps, perhaps not. The specialist might have quoted a 50 percent contingency fee anyway. But with such a good case, the clients could have shopped it to other damage suit specialists and gotten the percentage down, perhaps to only 25 percent of the recovery.

The clients could also have agreed to, say, a 35 percent fee, 25 percent to the specialist and 10 percent ($40,000 in this case) to the lawyer who "discovered" their case and got them a good lawyer to handle it. That's still a chunk of change for a morning's work. So, maybe the clients might also have required the forwarding lawyer to stay in the case as their adviser or "watchdog" over the specialist. That is an extension of the way to use a general practitioner or a lawyer-broker, mentioned in Chapter 7.

LAWYER-BROKERS

I suggested in Chapter 7 that you might come out better using a lawyer-broker to give you a list of specialists for your type of case. You can also use a lawyer-broker to negotiate the specialist's fee, or at least to give you a range of what to expect. Furthermore, you can use a lawyer-broker to monitor the specialist's work.

For instance, if your case is the kind that lends itself to an hourly rate or flat fee arrangement, your lawyer-broker should be able to tell you approximately what the specialist's fee should be. He should also agree to consult further with you if you have a problem with the specialist he recommends.

For instance, I recently referred a client to a lawyer colleague for a divorce. I told her that he would charge her about $2,000 for her part of it. She met with him one time, and he drew up the lawsuit papers. Then she and her husband got back together. The lawyer sent her a bill for $350, which seemed high to her, so she called me. I thought the bill was high, too, and called the lawyer. He cut it to $150.

Things are a bit different if your case is a damage suit. Normally, a lawyer will expect to receive a fat forwarding fee from the specialist he selects. Seldom will a forwarding lawyer negotiate the specialist's fee for you. One reason he won't is that by doing so, he reduces his referral fee. Another reason is that members of the brotherhood often view each other's fees as not open to discussion. So here's how to do it.

Tell your lawyer-broker that you, not the specialist, will give him, say, 10 percent of the recovery. For that he will select a specialist suitable to you, negotiate the specialist's fee to rock bottom and stay in the case as your watchdog adviser over the specialist's work and the case. If the lawyer-broker doesn't like that approach, say that you simply want him to earn his fee, rather than having it given to him by a specialist. If that doesn't get his attention, tell him you will use another lawyer. If your case is any size at all, he will tell you what a great idea lawyer brokering is.

What about the specialist? How will he react to being monitored by another lawyer? Not very well, at first. Then he will get out his calculator and figure out what 25 percent of your case might be worth. From that point on, you should have smooth sailing with him, too. If not, your lawyer-broker can step in and try to resolve any problems that come up.

For example, I once referred the wife of a client to a damage suit specialist. My friend's wife had been injured in an automobile accident. The case was settled and the specialist tried to pay all of his expenses out of my client's share of the recovery. I was present at the time of settlement and suggested that since the specialist was working on a 30 percent contingency, he should pick up 30 percent of the costs. He quickly agreed to do this because I had sent him several other good cases in the past, and he wanted me to send more in the future.

Once you reach a fee agreement with your lawyer, it's time to:

PUT IT IN WRITING

Putting the fee arrangement in writing cannot be overemphasized. Verbal fee agreements, while legal, are very difficult to prove. Furthermore, if it's in writing, you avoid the risk of a "misunderstanding" later on, or a shock (on your part).

For example, there's a very good firm in my city that represents a lot of wealthy people. I know that they seldom put their fee agreements in writing—for good reason, too. If their clients knew what the fee was going to be up front, they would faint. The firm knows that and delays the surprise until after the work is done. The client is then presented with the whopping bill. That is another example of the horse being out of the barn. If you don't put it in writing, you are asking for it.

RENEGOTIATING THE CONTINGENCY FEE

The following tidbit of information could save you a lot of money if your lawyer is working on a contingency basis in a damage suit. Assume that the defendant has offered $50,000, and you want $60,000 and not a penny less. The defendant's offer is "final." Consider offering to come down $3,000, if your lawyer will give up the same and get the defendant up $4,000. If the defendant won't budge, then offer to come down $5,000 if your lawyer will reduce his fee $5,000. Damage suit lawyers do that more often than you might think. The ploy works best deep in the negotiations, when the other side has made its "last" offer—and your lawyer is hungry or fed up with you or your case.

SETTLING UP

When it's all over, you should meet with the lawyer and discuss his final bill or contingency fee, whichever is appropriate. He should give you a written statement explaining his fee charges and itemizing any costs he has incurred on your behalf. Depending on how involved the case was, you may want to see the backup information (bills) for the costs. If the lawyer worked by the hour and the fee is large, ask to see his timesheets. He should be able to give you a handwritten time summary or computer printout and the backup on the expenses immediately. If he can't, how was he able to figure the bill? Do not let him know ahead of time that you are going to ask for this. If he can't prove his fee and/or expenses, don't pay the bill.

If the lawyer worked on a contingency basis and the expenses are high, ask the lawyer to share them with you instead of taking them out of your portion of the recovery. After all, you were in partnership together, with, say, 35 percent of the action for him and 65 percent for you. Shouldn't he share 35 percent of the costs of the venture? To guarantee that result, it should be part of your original, written agreement. But, if you are reading this after hiring your lawyer, you still might be able to get him to agree to it. Remember, he wants to keep your goodwill and get referrals from you in the future.

SUMMATION

We have covered a lot in this chapter. I held the war stories to a minimum because there was so much hard information to convey. Some of the ideas presented are going to be new to the lawyers you encounter. They may resist your efforts in many cases. Don't give up. Don't be timid. Do be polite. And keep in mind at all times that it's *your* case, and you are entitled to the best representation at the least cost that you can obtain.

I know a lawyer who says the following about his bills: "If my clients don't squawk about them, then I know I didn't charge enough." You don't have to put up with this charge-what-the-traffic-will-bear attitude if you don't want to.

Next, let's look at how to get along with your lawyer.

9

Your Lawyer and You

THE VARIOUS TALES and examples presented up to now were meant to teach you what to expect from a good lawyer and what to look for in a bad one. Hopefully, your antenna will be more sensitive as a result. Of course, you will want your lawyer to be a strong advocate, as well as a wise, no-nonsense adviser. But there's a lot more to having a successful relationship with your lawyer. For example, I feel that it's just as important for you and your lawyer to like each other as it is for you to have the "best" lawyer in town.

COMPATIBILITY

Suppose, for example, that you are a conservative person in thought and dress. You have a good damage suit and are referred to a killer type of plaintiff's attorney. He meets you in his office dressed in a white suit, black shirt, wearing diamond rings and a gold necklace. Think you will like that arrangement?

Or, suppose you are an insecure type of person, in need of constant attention. You are referred by a friend to a no-nonsense lawyer, one who doesn't like to do a lot of hand-holding. Do yourself a favor. Get another lawyer.

COMPASSION

Simply liking your lawyer isn't always enough. Lawyers often deal with tough problems, and, as a result, they often see clients at their worst. Such cases require a lot of patience on the lawyer's part if the lawyer and client are to get along with each other.

For instance, in Chapter 6 I related the story of a divorce case where I represented the wife. The first day she came into my office, an absolute wreck, physically and mentally. Her case lasted months, and we spent long hours together, preparing for the various hearings and just talking. Besides being her lawyer, I spent a lot of time trying to be her friend—and her psychologist. I never got paid for all of the time that I spent with her, but I felt good knowing that I had helped her through a really bad time.

My former law professor, Sam Beatty, told my class: "Being a lawyer is the second toughest profession in the world. The toughest is being a minister." After handling a few cases like that of my divorce client, I better understood what he meant. A lot of lawyering is just being a good listener and a friend. Most people need a lawyer with those qualities.

Another important aspect of the lawyer-client relationship is being honest with your lawyer. And usually, you can be. Here's why.

CONFIDENTIALITY

Your lawyer is required by his code of ethics to keep strictly to himself anything you tell him in confidence—unless, of course, you authorize its disclosure. For instance, I know a lawyer who will not even disclose the names of his clients. But let me tell you a story (which I read about in a legal publication) that even more graphically demonstrates this rule.

A lawyer had requested an ethics ruling based on the following situation. A valued employee of one of the lawyer's corporate clients secretly decided to go into business for himself, in direct competition with his employer. Part of his plan was to take a few of his employer's best employees. Having previously had good dealings with his employer's lawyer, the employee sought the latter's help in setting up the new business. The lawyer, after hearing the plan, had to decline because there would be a conflict of interest.

Naturally, the lawyer had a burning desire to tell his corporate client what was afoot, but he was concerned about violating the confidentiality rule if he blew the whistle. Instead he requested an ethics ruling from his bar association. The response was that since the employee came to him in confidence, he could not disclose anything.

Of course, not all lawyers would follow the rule that closely in a situation such as the one presented in the example. And I cannot help but think that the employee was just plain dumb to take his plan of revolt to his employer's lawyer. I would *never* confide in a lawyer who has a conflict of interest between me and my adversary.

There are special problems in criminal cases. Normally, a lawyer cannot reveal anything his criminal client says or does. However, a lawyer must inform the authorities if he knows that his client plans to commit *another* crime. Furthermore, recent cases and rule changes prohibit defense lawyers from advising criminal clients about how to destroy damaging evidence. And, if a lawyer comes into possession of damaging evidence, such as the murder weapon, cash received in a drug deal, or a corporation's double set of books in an income tax evasion case, then the lawyer may face criminal penalties himself for not turning such evidence over to the authorities.

HONESTY

The confidentiality rule usually allows you to be honest with your lawyer. If you aren't, you may well regret it. For instance, how can your lawyer accurately evaluate your case without seeing all of your cards? Take the following example as proof.

I once represented a woman in what appeared to be a very good harassment case. She claimed that she had not been paid money she had earned on her job because she would not play bedtime games with her boss. She told me that the problem began after she visited his apartment at his insistence, from which she was forced to flee to preserve her virtue. The business records indicated she was due what she claimed, and we stood to recover that plus punitive damages, which are awarded over actual damages when a defendant has acted in bad faith or despicably.

The case was out of my area of work, so I referred her to another lawyer who specialized in unusual damage suits. After he filed the lawsuit, the other side took our client's deposition (sworn out-of-court testimony) to see what she had to say. She repeated what she had told me and the specialist, with some *minor* embellishments.

Before fleeing on the fateful evening, she had given her boss a very esoteric type of foot massage called "reflexology." She went into great detail explaining how each portion of the foot corresponded to a different gland, organ, or other part of the body, and that by massaging a part of the foot, you in effect massaged the corresponding part of the body. She didn't go so far as to say what part of his body she was trying to massage on his foot, but I had a pretty good idea. In any event, you could understand how her boss might have been disappointed when she ran out just when he was being "relaxed."

The effect of that startling disclosure was to kill the punitive damage claim and to cause the specialist to resign from the case. Later, when I asked her why she had not mentioned the massage to me, she said, "I didn't think it was important." Had I known the truth, I could have settled the case myself without filing the lawsuit. The client was more interested in revenge, though, than justice.

I could tell you fifty more stories just like that one and so could every lawyer I know. The moral is be honest with your lawyer, or at least tell him what the other side knows about you.

LAWYER COMMUNICATION

By far, the most frequent cause of grievances and malpractice suits filed against lawyers is poor communication with clients. Lawyers are told that constantly by their bar associations and malpractice insurance carriers. Yet they still don't communicate well. Therefore, you should insist on getting copies of everything the lawyer does himself or gets from other lawyers or the court. You should also call your lawyer about once a month to be brought up to date. Otherwise, you will almost surely become dissatisfied with your lawyer's performance, even if it's otherwise outstanding.

If you have anything important to tell your lawyer, try to do it in writing. There are several reasons for doing this. First, a written communication (if it isn't too long and involved) is more attention-getting. Second, busy lawyers often forget to write down what you tell them—either in the office or on the telephone. Third, it's the only way you can prove what you told your lawyer if a problem develops between the two of you. For that reason, you should be sure to keep copies of everything you give your lawyer, as well as anything you get from him. Use a legal file or a notebook, just as a lawyer does. He has a file on you, and you should have one on him.

Another problem clients often experience is not understanding what their lawyer will do in the case or how long it will take. Before any work is done, your lawyer should explain to you what he's going to do. For instance, if he's to write your will or draw up a partnership agreement, he should estimate the number of meetings you will have, outline the substance of the documents, and give you a completion date. If instead your case is a lawsuit, then he should tell you about the costs you are likely to incur, what will be involved in trying the case, how long it might take (at the outside), and his opinion of the outcome (good or bad).

If your lawyer is less optimistic about the case than you, that is a *good* sign. It means that he is looking at the case realistically, something you probably will not be able to do at the outset. Be very wary of any lawyer who is not more pessimistic about your case than are you. Such a lawyer either does not know how to evaluate a case or is telling you what you want to hear to get you to use him. In other words, he is either a "boaster" or a "Dale Carnegie" lawyer.

Another big communication problem is the lawyer's fee, which was discussed in Chapter 8. Understand that many lawyers are reluctant to discuss fees or to set an exact amount. If your lawyer won't do this, you are going to have a problem later. Count on it. That brings me to my last point in the communications area.

Get your lawyer to put in writing all of the above. If you don't, a "misunderstanding" in the lawyer's favor could develop, and it's very hard to prove what he *said* he would do or would charge you. Don't pay him or let him start work until you have this in hand.

HOMEWORK

Even though you are paying your lawyer to do the work, he probably will ask you to do homework. For instance, if you have been damaged physically (say in an automobile accident) or economically (say by breach of contract) your lawyer should ask you to write a "short story" about your case. The story should contain the following information in the order of occurrence: how it started, what happened, and the outcome; the names, addresses, and telephone numbers of everyone involved; what everyone said and who heard it; what written documents are involved (furnish copies of them, keeping the originals in a safe place); how the event affected you when it occurred and affects you now, i.e., how you feel, sleep, get along with others, and so forth. You will save time by having written your short story and arranged your documents before you even interview the lawyer the first time.

If your case will involve litigation (a lawsuit), there's a related problem.

WITNESS PREPARATION

Your lawyer should not wait until the last minute to prepare you or your witnesses for trial (or interview the other side's witnesses). The more complex or expensive the case, the more time should be put into this. You can tell if your lawyer is doing this correctly by whether you and your witnesses spend long, grueling sessions with him, where he will doubt everything you say, as if he were the other side's lawyer. He will tell you to answer his questions instead of saying what you think he wants to hear—or trying to say it so that the other side can't use it against you. If you don't get mad at him in these sessions, then he's not doing it right.

In a really important case, the lawyer should bring in another lawyer to "cross-examine" you, just as if it's a real trial. He may even conduct a mock trial with jurors—to make sure your testimony is clear and unassailable. I would even suggest that your practice testimony, in an important case, be videotaped and reviewed by you. Then you will see what it is you aren't doing right and correct it.

If the other side asks to take the depositions of you or your witnesses before the trial, then your lawyer should spend a lot of time preparing you and your witnesses. If he doesn't, something may be said that could severely damage your case—something that perhaps could have been said a little differently without causing any injury.

If you were an actor and the courtroom a stage, you would have several rehearsals, then a last dress rehearsal. The same applies to witness preparation. You and your witnesses are *not* being taught to lie—only to present the facts in the most favorable light to you. If this bothers you, rest assured that the other side is doing it, too, and that if you or your witnesses aren't ready, your case may be destroyed on cross-examination by the other side's lawyer.

If your case is important, your lawyer, besides interviewing the other side's witnesses, should take their depositions. This will cost some money, but the cost is usually worth what you stand to gain. For instance, something very favorable to your case may be said, or perhaps you will find out that your case is weaker than you thought and that you should try to settle it.

Now let's look at another important aspect of the relationship.

WHO DECIDES?

One of your lawyer's duties to you is to play devil's advocate—argue with you—during the advising process. However, when it comes down to *deciding* the course of action, that you must do, since you, not your lawyer, will have to live with the outcome. As with clients who would not come clean, I've had a lot of clients who would not make a decision. And so has every lawyer I know. That brings up a related subject.

LISTEN TO YOUR LAWYER

Although you are the one who makes the decisions, it is your lawyer who advises you as to what he believes, based on his experience, is the best course for you to follow. In Chapter 6, I related the story of the young man who bought a business against his lawyer's warning, then went broke. Let me give you another example.

I was acting as the court-appointed representative of a teenage boy whose parents had been killed by a drunk who was driving on the wrong side of the highway. His sister had assumed legal guardianship over him until he was of legal age. A large damage suit had been filed on behalf of their deceased parents' estate, and they stood to come into a lot of money.

Knowing that money was on the way, the boy's sister decided he needed a new car in place of his old, but perfectly functional, Volkswagen. She called the estate's lawyer and told him that she wanted to get her brother a $17,000 Honda, using the VW as a trade-in vehicle. She wanted the estate to reimburse her out of her brother's inheritance for the difference between $17,000 and the trade-in amount ($2,500). The lawyer advised her to let him get the court to approve it first. But she was in a hurry and bought the Honda anyway. She then came back to the lawyer and asked him to request that the court order the reimbursement. Title to the car was in the sister's name for insurance purposes (she said).

As the boy's representative, I was forced to tell the judge that I didn't think the facts justified the type of expenditure involved. The judge was already of the same view. The sister cornered me out in the hall and tried to browbeat me into going along with her request. My job was to protect the boy's assets, and I told her that I simply could not agree to her demands. Then she cried, to no avail.

In the end, we settled on a $3,000 reimbursement, which, when added to the $2,500 trade-in on the VW, would have bought a nice $5,500 used car—about what the judge and I felt the facts warranted. The sister was forced to wait until her brother reached legal age to find out if he would repay the balance of $11,500 ($17,000 − $5,500). She should have listened to her lawyer.

Another problem that often develops in the relationship is that the client feels that the lawyer is never available.

YOU AREN'T YOUR LAWYER'S ONLY CLIENT

If your lawyer is any good, he will have a lot of clients. So, while you will be important to him, he usually will not be available whenever—or as much as—you want to see him. If you feel it's important that you get together, make an office appointment. Don't call to chat on the telephone. Telephones are for making appointments or other brief messages (usually), not making important decisions or working on your case. And remember, if your lawyer is working by the hour, he will bill you for telephone calls. If you can't get an appointment for several days, don't get paranoid—unless you've been a nag. Then you can be paranoid. Otherwise, rest assured that your lawyer is not ignoring you—that he's working on his other clients' cases, which are as important to them as yours is to you. He works on yours just as hard, too.

Now let's examine one more area that often causes problems.

DOING BUSINESS TOGETHER

Lawyers sometimes end up doing business with their clients outside of the lawyer/client relationship. Often this occurs when the lawyer does work for a client, for example, by putting together a business or investment deal, and the lawyer takes back an ownership interest for his fee. Less commonly, the lawyer will actually put money into a client's deal. In either case, the lawyer has a potential, if not actual, conflict of interest with you. If the business venture goes sour, you will have an adversary handling your legal affairs. Regardless, you will be stuck in an uncomfortable business relationship. For those reasons, it is wise to avoid doing business with your lawyer.

SUMMATION

A good way to look at the relationship with your lawyer is as if it were a partnership—perhaps even a marriage. After an initial courtship, you get to know each other well. Eventually, you are able to read each other's moods or even minds. And that's the way it should be. In the next chapter, I will tell some stories about clients who didn't understand that.

10

Don't Kill Your Lawyer

IN THE OPENING REMARKS, I said I wasn't going to kill all of the lawyers—that while some might need killing, many didn't. The lawyers in Chapters 1 through 4 are the ones that I killed for you. If any others die, it will be at your own hands, and you probably will suffer for it.

This chapter relates several stories about clients who "killed" their lawyers. The result in each case was that the lawyer tended to be "in court" whenever the client called or came by, and the case did not turn out as well as the client had hoped.

Theoretically, a lawyer should not let the kinds of things about to be presented affect his advocacy. However, most lawyers are human (I think) and have many of the same weaknesses that you do. Remember, as you read what follows, that the lawyer-client relationship is a partnership—a marriage, so to speak—between you and your lawyer. If you abuse your lawyer, then the relationship (and your case) may suffer.

CLIENTS WHO DON'T PAY

Not long after I started practicing law, a home builder hired me to defend a lawsuit that had been filed against him by a dissatisfied customer. I quoted a fee and he agreed to it. The fee was to be paid in stages, the last part of it the week before the trial. The money dribbled in here and there, always less than scheduled, always late. I saw the handwriting on the wall and wrote him a letter saying that if the balance wasn't paid by trial day, I would withdraw from the case. He called and said not to worry, that I would be paid by then.

When we met at the courthouse, I still had not been paid, and he didn't have the money with him. I was infuriated and told the judge that I was withdrawing from the case for nonpayment of my fee. It was unethical of me to do this on the trial day, because my client was left without a lawyer at the last minute. The correct approach would have been to ask the court for permission to withdraw several weeks before the case was to be tried. This would have given my client time to arrange for another lawyer to come into the case.

Seeing how mad I was, the wise judge knew that my client would be better off without me. So I was allowed to withdraw, and my client had to find another lawyer to make arrangements to try the case another day. While I was prepared to be his knight in shining armor, his behavior got the best of me, and I behaved awfully.

DISHONEST CLIENTS

In Chapter 9, I related the story of a client who didn't tell me about giving her boss a foot massage until the other side took her deposition. At that point, I realized the case wasn't worth anywhere near what I had first thought and that my client's real motive was to use me to beat up on her boss with a lawsuit. As you can imagine, my interest in her case waned after the deposition.

The case had another interesting twist, though. After realizing I wasn't going to be her pawn anymore, my client went to the other side and attempted to settle part of the case without me. The other side's lawyer, being a member in good standing of the lawyer brotherhood, told her he wasn't going to be a party to that sort of thing and alerted me to what was going on. Needless to say, I didn't put much more effort into the settlement negotiations. Nor will I ever represent her again.

UNCOOPERATIVE CLIENTS

Uncooperative clients do everything possible to prevent you from helping them. For example, a woman went to a lawyer friend of mine after her divorce. The client had been awarded a fine home and was in the process of selling it. My friend could see that she didn't have a lick of business sense and that she needed someone to help her preserve her assets, or she would waste them and end up destitute. She also was experiencing a sexual renaissance, and was seeing a lot of men. He was concerned that she would set up house with one of them, which, under state law, would give her ex-husband grounds to have his alimony payments to her stopped—permanently.

Try as he might, my friend couldn't control her. One day, she came in to tell him about her latest skiing trip to Colorado; the next week, she brought by a new Ford Thunderbird for him to admire. She got into metaphysics (spiritualism) and brought him volumes of reading material on that; she dropped in whenever she felt like it. All the while, he wasn't charging her because of her deteriorating situation. If he had, it might have gotten her attention.

Finally, her financial position reached the bottom, and she asked my friend to file a suit to increase her alimony. He did this, then regretted it. Her unexpected visits to his office doubled in frequency. He was forced time after time to relive her divorce and hear how everyone but she was the cause of her problems. He had to start fending off her creditors, one of which was the IRS. She hadn't filed a tax return for two years.

Then, the worst thing imaginable happened. Her ex-husband proved that she was living with another man. (She hadn't told my friend.) Instead of getting more alimony, she ended up with none. My friend didn't get paid. And the last time my friend saw his client, she was talking to nonexistent beings.

OPPRESSIVE CLIENTS

Oppressive clients think they know more about handling a lawsuit than the lawyer does. In fact, if permitted, these clients assume all responsibility for planning and preparing the case, then sit beside the lawyer at the trial passing a flood of notes and constantly whispering in the lawyer's ear, telling him what to do next.

For example, a man once came to me about suing another lawyer for botching a bankruptcy case. I told him that I would investigate the case at an hourly rate with a $500 retainer. I would then tell him if I was interested in the case. Right off, he started trying to get me to take the case in any event and to put a cap on my fee. I told him that, *if* I liked what I saw and *if* I decided to take his case, then I would handle it on a certain percentage. Apparently, he didn't hear the "ifs," as I later learned to my rue. I also asked him to write me a brief summary of the facts and what he thought his lawyer had done wrong. He left in good spirits, and I started looking over the documents he had left with me.

Within a week, I received in the mail a document of about fifty pages, entitled "Brief of the Law and Facts"—the homework I had given him. It was impossibly long and involved and convoluted in reasoning. I knew that I was in trouble. Well, I waded through it all and came to this conclusion: His lawyer was indeed guilty of malpractice. However, half of the blame lay on our mutual client, who had been so oppressive and meddlesome that the lawyer had lost interest in the case—in fact, he was repulsed by it. While my client would have the best of the legal argument, he would be penalized for his oppressive and meddlesome behavior. The jury would sympathize with the first lawyer and reduce the damages accordingly.

As you can imagine, my client didn't receive my analysis very well. Then, when I told him that the case was too "iffy" for me to handle on a contingency—that I would only do it on an hourly fee basis with a substantial retainer—he went wild. "We made a deal!" he screamed. "Now you're reneging. It's a great case, anyway—I don't agree with your analysis." And so it went for the better part of an hour and several later meetings. By then, I was determined not to take the case under any circumstances and made myself more difficult for him to reach. Eventually, he stopped trying to convert me and picked up his file. I fully expected him to file a grievance against me. Fortunately, he didn't.

POSSESSIVE CLIENTS

Related to the oppressive client is the possessive client—one who thinks his is the only case you are working on or should be. For instance, I know of an antitrust case that has been going on for over a decade. The plaintiff's lawyer, I'm sure, never dreamed he would handle a case of that duration. The theory of the case has changed several times during the time it has been in court. The plaintiff has set up his own office inside the lawyer's offices. From there, he does legal research, uses the lawyer's secretary and telephones, and plans his strategy. The lawyer is like an organ grinder's monkey, doing his master's bidding.

MOANERS

Another aggravating client is the moaner—the person who enjoys complaining about life more than solving its problems. For example, a lawyer friend of mine once had an aftermath divorce client. She didn't use him for the divorce, but came to him later—after she had worn out her first lawyer.

Her ex-husband was "harassing" her on the telephone, and she wanted my friend to bring a lawsuit to ask a judge to order him to leave her alone. My friend told her that such orders usually were worth only the paper they were written on, but that he would file the suit on payment of a $500 retainer. Of course, she wanted him to file it for nothing and then ask the court to order the ex-husband to pay his fee, which he wasn't inclined to do. So, she left unhappy.

Nevertheless, she started calling my friend every time her ex called her. Finally, he told her that he could solve her problem. She asked how, and he said that first she would have to promise to do what he would suggest. Well, she wasn't about to do that, and things rocked along as before for a while. Eventually, though, her curiosity got the best of her, and she called to find out what he wanted her to do. Again, he told her that she would first have to promise to do it. And again she balked.

"What's the matter? Don't you really want to stop his calls?" my friend asked. She didn't reply. "Just as I thought. Call me when you are serious," he said.

"Wait a minute, I'll do it," she said, not sounding very happy. He told her to tell her ex, the next time he called, that she wasn't going to talk to him on the telephone anymore—that she would, in the future, hang up as soon as she heard his voice. And to do it.

"But what if he's calling about the children?" she whined.

"Tell him to write you a letter or to call them, not you," he replied.

Silence.

"It'll work; I guarantee it," he said.

Still silence.

"What's the matter? You getting some kind of perverted pleasure out of his calls?" he taunted.

"Of course not," she snapped.

"Well, how long do these conversations last?" he asked.

"Oh, some last as long as forty-five minutes. It's unbearable," she moaned.

"Does he do all the talking?" he asked.

"No, of course not!" she replied.

"Well, you take part in the conversation then?"

"Of course!"

"Why, if it's driving you nuts?" he taunted again.

"Well . . . oh, I don't know!" she said angrily.

"Oh, I think you do," he said.

Eventually, she agreed to try my friend's suggestion, and they ended the conversation. Her file came up for review a month later, and, not having heard from her, he called to see what had happened.

"Well, I tried what you suggested," she said.

"And?"

"He got mad as hell."

"So what? You weren't expecting him to bring roses, were you? Anything else happen?"

"Well, he tried to call several times, and after a while, he got tired of me hanging up and he quit calling me."

"Well, didn't that make you happy? It's what you wanted, wasn't it?" he asked.

"Yeah, I guess so," she said reluctantly.

Care to guess how long it took her to pay his fee?

AVENGERS

An avenger is the client who is more interested in using the lawyer as a weapon to punish the other side than in justice or resolution of the problem. The client in the last example was also an avenger—preferring a full-blown lawsuit to a simple practical solution. As was my client who was into foot massage. If I realize up front that I'm dealing with an avenger, I quote a healthy retainer and an hourly fee. That usually cools them off. If not, at least I know I'm getting paid. Avengers eventually turn on their lawyers, too, as did those two clients.

DESTROYERS

Destroyers are the types who have a good case but go out of the way to lose it. For instance, I was representing a man against his company. He had suffered a heart attack and was fired before he could return to work. The real reason he was fired was because he was an alcoholic and had said some things to his boss that he shouldn't have at a company party.

The suit was filed because the company wouldn't assist in processing his medical insurance claims, nor would it pay his unemployment benefits due under his employment agreement. Besides claiming the unpaid insurance and benefits, we were also asking for punitive damages. Our theory for winning was that his boss was improperly punishing him for his alcoholism and smart remarks.

Several of our key witnesses were employees and doctors of the hospital where my client had been treated for alcoholism. We needed them to prove he was an alcoholic and not responsible for his actions. Unfortunately, his wife took up a crusade against alcoholism and carried this to the employees and doctors we needed as witnesses. She wore out her welcome with them, which I learned about in time to repair the damage. However, I couldn't control her, and she kept calling and berating my witnesses. Finally, I wrote her and her husband a letter warning her to cease and desist. Otherwise, I would resign from the case. She didn't, and I filed a motion with the judge asking to be allowed to withdraw (by now, I knew the right way to do this). To my utter surprise, she and her husband wrote the judge asking that I be required to stay on the case. He saw the futility of forcing a reluctant lawyer to represent a beast of a client and let me resign. I fully expected to be sued or have a grievance filed against me. And I was surprised when it didn't happen.

Now let's look at one more lawyer killer.

SMART ASSES

This was my first bad experience with a client. He was being threatened with criminal prosecution for the theft of a very large diamond ring, which he vigorously denied stealing. After being sent off on several wild goose hunts to interview alibi witnesses, I met with and told him to cut the B.S. and tell me what really happened. After a lot of squirming, he admitted the theft. I told him to bring me the ring so that I could return it to its owner's lawyer and stop the arrest warrant from being issued. He agreed to do this and left.

The next day he returned with a ring and left it with my secretary—I was out at the time. On returning, I called the owner's lawyer and made arrangements to deliver the ring right away. When I gave the ring to him, he pulled out a jeweler's glass (to my amazement) and examined the ring. Then he doubled up in laughter.

"It's a yag!" he said.

"What's that?" I asked.

"A piece of glass, dumbo."

Shortly afterward, my client and I had a very interesting meeting at which I doubled my fee. The real stone was eventually returned, but whenever I see that lawyer, he always teases me about what a dupe I was.

SUMMATION

The cases in this chapter are representative of lawyer killers—the kind of people lawyers pray never to have as clients. If you saw yourself in this chapter, then you probably will have a bad experience with your lawyer. This brings us to the end of the discussion about having a successful relationship with your lawyer. In Part III, you will learn a lot about lawsuits and why it's usually best to try to avoid them.

PART III

COURT BATTLES

11

The Hazards of Litigation

THIS CHAPTER IS for the reader who's facing a lawsuit or defending criminal charges. The unpredictability and costs or, as lawyers say, the hazards of litigation are not necessarily good for your health, as you shall soon see. But first, some philosophy.

In the old days, if someone made you mad, you could either talk it out, turn the other cheek, or square off and settle your differences with your bare hands, sticks, swords, pistols, or whatever was in vogue at that time in history. There were no lawyers to hire, no judges or juries nearby to decide who was to win or lose and no long waits for a decision. The outcome, though not always producing justice, was swift and usually final.

That "uncivilized" way of physically resolving disputes is generally now out of favor, although you do see throwbacks to it from time to time around beer halls, truck stops, after the play is over in professional football games, and, oh yes, in movies or television and in the news. For the rest of us, there are rules requiring that we take our unresolved disputes to the courts, where "wise" judges and juries, with the able assistance of highly evolved lawyers, help us work things out. In *theory*, justice is now served, albeit very slowly. In actuality, I'm not sure justice is served. But, even if it is, you seldom come away from the courthouse with the same feeling of satisfaction that you would have gotten by punching the other side in the nose.

THE FINANCIAL COST

America is the most litigious (suit-happy) country in the world. The "sue-the-bastards" mentality has gone way beyond the realm of shysters. The history of American lawyers is like the history of labor unions or government welfare programs. In the beginning, there was a crying need for them. Now, it seems that they are running amok.

Many, many times I have been called by people threatened with being sued. They tell me their side of the case in the most favorable light that they can, leaving the other side with no apparent legal leg to stand on. I tell them that, based on what they have told me, they are in the right.

"Then they can't sue me!" they assert.

"I didn't say that," I say.

"But you said that I was in the right, didn't you?" they demand.

"Yes, but that doesn't mean they can't sue you just the same," I say to their shock.

The sad fact is that anybody can sue you for anything, without any legal justification. Such cases are often called harassment or nuisance suits. You have to defend the suit. If you win, then you may be able to sue the other side or their lawyer for abusive litigation—and wait three years or so for a trial and your "justice."

The simplest and fairest way to reduce the amount and thus the costs of litigation would be to adopt the "English Rule," under which the loser of a lawsuit must pay the winner's legal expenses. In England plaintiffs think long and hard about bringing weak suits, and defendants are less inclined to stall (and hence increase the cost of) cases they can't win. Of course, the adoption of such a system in America would put quite a few lawyers out of work, which may be why the idea hasn't gotten very far. So, as things now stand, the first hazard of litigation is the cost (unless an insurance company is paying your lawyer). As Voltaire once said: "I was ruined twice in my life—once when I lost a lawsuit and once when I won one."

THERE ARE NO WINNERS

A plaintiff in my city recently won a $6 million award for injuries received in an accident that cost him two arms and a leg. How do you think all of that money made him feel? Or what about your best friend who just hammered his or her spouse in a divorce? Is your friend really happy now? Probably not. Even most winners in divorce cases are left with long-lasting emotional, if not financial, scars.

Take a civil (noncriminal) case. You, the plaintiff, win. Still, you aren't put back in your original position. The courts simply cannot restore eyesight lost in a job accident, rejuvenate a business destroyed by unfair competition, or return the sense of well-being lost in the breakdown of a marriage. No amount of money can do that.

And what money you do receive often must be shared with your lawyer.

If, on the other hand, you are the defendant and win, you still lose. Besides being out the legal costs in a civil suit, it will be a long time before you get over the emotional trauma and the threat of financial ruin caused by the lawsuit. Or, if you successfully defend a criminal case, acquittal will not repay your legal fees or restore your reputation. There will always be those who wonder if you really did it. And I doubt you will ever get over the emotional trauma suffered by you and your family.

Each of these examples shows that there are usually no winners in litigation except, perhaps, the trial lawyers.

CLOGGED DOCKETS

If you have a serious civil case—one that is not a candidate for the small claims court—then you are going to be in for a rude awakening when you sit down with your lawyer. That's when you will learn that, good as your case is, it will be many months, perhaps even years, before it's ever set for trial. There probably will also be several continuances before it is actually tried. In the meantime? Find something else to worry about. There will be very little that your lawyer can do to speed things up in court.

Because of the delay, many plaintiffs seeking to recover damages end up settling their cases for less than they are worth, simply to get something coming in—or just to get out from under the agony of waiting and not knowing how the case will turn out. And if the plaintiff's lawyer is hungry, he will push his client in this direction.

Defense lawyers are well aware of the tendency on the part of plaintiffs and their lawyers to settle early, and they use it to save their defendant clients money. In other words, were you the plaintiff, they would just wait you (or your lawyer) out. Stalling also allows the defendant to hang on to his or her money longer and earn interest on it. And there's one other reason defense lawyers stall—something may happen to reduce the value of your case. For example, a person paralyzed in an automobile accident and facing a lingering existence and huge medical and nursing bills may die. That eliminates a major portion of the damages that the defendant will have to pay.

Or take this case. You buy a home with a serious defect—the septic system malfunctions in wet weather. So, you sue the seller for the cost of replacing it and for punitive damages because he did not tell you about it. A year later, you are transferred by your employer to another state. Continuing the lawsuit will be more expensive and troublesome. You slowly lose interest in it for that reason and for the further reason that you no longer have to smell the problem when it rains. So, you settle for less.

If you are a defendant in a criminal case, the delay also can work to your advantage. A key witness may die or move away. The red-hot D.A. assigned to your case may get hired by a private law firm, and his replacement is likely to be green, perhaps fresh out of law school. You now have a better chance of winning or getting a decent settlement offer.

The long and the short of it is this: Delay hurts plaintiffs and helps defendants. That's why most big settlements in plaintiffs' cases occur literally on the courthouse steps the day the case is set for trial—or even during the trial. Only at this point have you proven to the defense lawyer and defendant that you mean business—that you aren't going to sell out, which is why you should use an experienced *and* prosperous plaintiff's lawyer for a serious damage suit. Such a lawyer will not be in a hurry to settle and get something coming in for himself, meaning he will be in position to argue against your doing it, too.

LIABILITY

A serious hazard in a damage suit is being unable to prove that the defendant was at fault (did something wrong). You may have terrible injuries, but proving that the defendant was at fault (caused your injuries) may be very difficult to do. Take this example.

You are approaching an intersection in your automobile. As you enter the intersection, the light changes from green to yellow. At that instant, another vehicle crossing from your left collides with your car, causing you serious and permanent bodily injury. As you wait for the paramedics to put you in the ambulance, you try to remember what happened. All you can remember is the light turning from green to yellow as you entered the intersection. Then you hear the other driver telling the investigating police officer that you ran a red light. There are no other witnesses.

Later, when you meet with a plaintiff's lawyer and relate your sad story, you will be disappointed. "It's a swearing match," he will say, "your word against his. In fact, if he's right, then you owe *him* damages!"

Of course, if someone else had seen the accident and remembered that you had the light when you entered the intersection, then it would be a different matter. You would have an independent witness, whose testimony would not be tainted by personal gain, to testify for you.

In either scenario, you are in the right. However, in the first one, you will get a very low settlement offer and, if you don't settle, you may well lose the case altogether. In the second one, you will get a very good settlement offer, but if you try the case, you may hit the jackpot. I know this doesn't seem right, but you need to understand that that's the way it often happens.

Or take this example. A widow, whose husband had been killed in a private airplane crash, came to me. The pilot had been guilty of utterly reckless conduct. He wasn't instrument-rated, but had attempted an instrument landing under minimum conditions for such a landing, and he never advised the control tower that he wasn't instrument-rated. Of course, it was a great case against the pilot's estate (he was killed, too), but we felt there was a good case against the air traffic controller and the FAA (Federal Aviation Administration) as well. Here's why.

The FAA records on tape all pilot/controller communications. The insurance company defending the pilot's estate furnished us with the tape, which revealed that the air traffic controller knew that the pilot was flying his airplane in a dangerous fashion and did not have basic instrument landing maps for that airfield on board. On top of that, the controller was joking with someone else in the tower about the pilot's shortcomings. Our expert witness told us that the controller should have taken over, ordered the pilot to "maintain wings level," climb back to a safe altitude, and then question him about his instrument qualifications, which were clearly suspect. After learning the facts, the controller should then have directed the pilot with radar assistance to a field not under instrument conditions.

Well, that seemed like a good theory to us, but it got a lot better. When the FAA furnished us with the tape (they didn't know we already had it), the parts damaging to the FAA had been cut out of it, which made it look as if the FAA was hiding the truth and that they thought the same way as our expert. Making things even better was case law holding that whenever a party to a lawsuit tries to hide or destroy damaging evidence, the other side is entitled to the benefit of the doubt on what the evidence means. So, we felt that we had an open-and-shut case against the FAA as well.

But let me tell you something. There's no such thing as an open-and-shut case. The judge ruled against us on the issue of liability. Why? Because he felt that the pilot's acts were so reckless that it would not be fair to hold anyone else responsible. In legal jargon, the judge ruled that there was a "superseding cause" of the accident—the pilot's behavior—which wiped out the wrongful acts of the FAA controller. As a result, we got a big "donut," meaning nothing, from the FAA. To make matters worse, we had gotten a pretty good settlement offer from them during the trial, and, as lawyers say, "We left it (the offer) on the table."

DAMAGES

Besides proving liability, a plaintiff must also prove damages. Often it's clear that there are damages, but it's not clear how much they are worth. For instance, in the automobile intersection accident example mentioned before, it's simple enough to prove what hospital and nursing bills were, but how do you prove the amount of income you would lose in the future as a result of your injuries? Will you ever be able to go back to work? If so, when? If not, how much longer will you live, or, if you die, how much longer could your family have counted on your living and providing for them? Therefore, how do you measure the pain and suffering, mental anguish, or loss of the relationship with your spouse? Those questions have no clear-cut answers. All your lawyer can do is make an educated guess based on the results of similar cases.

Here's another example. You operate a small business selling auto parts. A national competitor sets up a store across the street and cuts its prices, below cost, eventually driving you out of business. You have a good unfair-competition case, but how do you figure what you have lost? What value can you put on the long hours that you put into building your business? How do you place a value on future earnings? Quantifying the damages is difficult—it's an art, not a science.

Now, let's look at a punitive damages case. A drunk driver crosses the median and hits you head-on, causing you serious injuries. Besides all of the standard damages, you now have a good case for punitive damages. Such damages may be awarded when a defendant has acted grossly—completely out of the realm of socially acceptable behavior. Other examples of punitive damages cases are fraud and intentional infliction of physical injury or property damage. Punitive damages are awarded for two reasons: first, to punish the defendant for his despicable behavior; second, to warn all others like him that they can expect the same treatment in the courts. To deter, in other words. Well, how do you measure the punitive damages in this case? You can't. Again, it's just an educated guess.

WITNESSES

Your witnesses can make or break your case. There's an old story about a lawyer who carefully interviewed a witness prior to trial. What the witness said was very favorable to the lawyer's client, so the lawyer decided to use the witness. However, during the trial, the witness told an entirely different version of what had happened, which severely damaged the case. After the trial was over, the lawyer called the witness to learn why he had changed his testimony. His answer: "When I was in your office, we were just talking; when I was in court, I was under oath."

Witnesses can lie in court, too. I remember a child visitation case in which the father had married a prostitute. The mother didn't want her son visiting his father when his new wife was around. My client brought the father's parents to my office, where they told me that they didn't want their grandson around their son's new wife either. I felt that their testimony would have a powerful impact on the judge and decided to call them as witnesses. At the trial, they backed their son and his new wife all the way. Since I, not their son's lawyer, had called them as witnesses, their adverse testimony hurt twice as much.

Not only do witnesses change their stories, they often just forget them. It's difficult to remember the fine details of a conversation that occurred months or even years ago. So, for all of the foregoing reasons, it's critical that your lawyer take *written* statements, signed by your witnesses as soon as possible. Having signed a written statement, they will be reluctant to change their stories. If they do, you can prove surprise (where a witness's testimony in court differs from what he or she told you earlier) and attack their testimony. Most courts will not allow you to attack your own witness's testimony, unless you can prove surprise.

Another problem with witnesses is that it's often difficult to get them to agree to come to court. I once tried a case in which my key witness was a former employee of my client and the defendant, who had been in business together. The witness, the wife of a lawyer, was afraid of the defendant and wouldn't agree to testify for us. I subpoenaed her. Her husband called and used threats to get me to withdraw the subpoena. I was unable to reason with him or get him to explain to his wife that I was just doing my job and that she had a legal and moral duty to testify. She eventually did testify, but I had to drag what I needed out of her. If the wife of a lawyer, whose cases often depend on a witness's testimony, was so uncooperative, think how other lay people behave when asked to testify. Most simply do not want to get involved.

TRIAL BY JURY OR BY JUDGE

If you don't want to settle, you can risk trying the case before either a jury or a judge, either of which may decide the case against you. Once you have the jury's verdict or judge's decision, prior offers of settlement go out the window.

Most damage suits are tried before a jury. Plaintiffs' lawyers prefer jury trials, because juries tend to side with the plaintiff in cases of questionable liability and give larger awards. Defense lawyers prefer trials by a judge for the opposite reasons. The U.S. and state constitutions provide for trial by jury in most types of civil cases. So, when the plaintiff's lawyer asks for a jury trial, the defense lawyer can't prevent it. However, there are cases that are tried only before judges, such as divorce, child custody, bankruptcy, injunctions (where you ask the court to order something to be done or stopped from being done), and most cases against the U.S. government.

If you are defending a criminal case, you want, and are entitled by right, to a jury trial. The D.A. has to prove guilt beyond a reasonable doubt to each juror. In effect, this gives you twelve chances to avoid conviction, since if just one juror refuses to convict you, the judge will order a mistrial. The D.A. must then decide whether to try you again or drop the case. Sometimes, when one or two jurors hold out for acquittal, the others get tired of the case and cross over. The result is a unanimous verdict for you, meaning you have won.

Once a case is decided, for or against you, by jury or judge, it's usually over. You don't get another chance—unless the judge or an appeals court later throws out the entire case because an error was made during the trial. (This is discussed more fully in Chapter 14.)

But let me once again point out that there is no such thing as an open-and-shut case. Any trial lawyer can tell you of a hundred cases that have surprised him—cases that left him wishing that he had taken the other side's settlement offer—or, in some cases, damn glad that he didn't.

SETTLEMENT OFFERS

In nearly all cases, the opposing sides will make what are called "settlement offers" to each other. The idea is to resolve the dispute between the parties, rather than allowing an unpredictable judge or jury to decide who gets what.

It is important for you to remember that rarely does either side get all that it wants when a case is settled. Nevertheless, you should seriously consider all settlement offers—especially those made on the courthouse steps or during a trial. This is when the other side will make its best offer to you in either a civil or criminal case. If the offer is close to what you are willing to take, then accept it. The hazard of losing a damage or other civil suit or being convicted of a greater crime in a criminal case is too much to gamble. However, if the offer is niggardly or downright insulting, then you probably have nothing to lose by going through with the trial.

Often a client is anxious to settle a case, but the other side is playing hard-to-get. If you are anxious, the best thing to do is back off. The worst thing to do is let the other side know that you are eager to settle. Once that happens, they will wait you out and get more from you than necessary.

In any event, it would be a very good idea to listen carefully to what your lawyer has to say at that point in time. If you've picked a good lawyer, the odds are that you will be a lot happier following his recommendation to accept or reject the offer than you will be if you don't.

One final suggestion here. If you do settle the case, put it in writing right then and there, get everyone to sign it (including the lawyers), and then give a copy of it to the judge for the court records. I've seen some real problems in cases where that wasn't done.

INSOLVENT DEFENDANTS

"You can't get blood out of a turnip," it's said. And if a defendant in a civil damage suit doesn't have any money or liability insurance, you won't get paid in all probability. Of course, the time to find out about the defendant's financial condition or insurance coverage is *before* you start a lawsuit. Lawyers, being interested in getting paid, are very good at doing that for you. If the defendant-to-be has no assets, why sue him and go through all the grief of a lawsuit?

There are, of course, exceptions to this advice. The defendant may be a "boom or bust" type. While he may be on hard times now, he may be flush later on.

Alternatively, insurance you carry may pay for your loss. For example, your neighbor chops down a tree and it lands on your house, but he doesn't have insurance and is otherwise unable to pay the damages. If you have homeowner's insurance, you will be reimbursed by your insurance carrier. Then, your insurance company will have to worry about collecting from your neighbor.

Or, suppose you are struck by an uninsured drunk driver. All states require that automobile insurance carriers provide what is called "uninsured motorist" coverage. There also is a minimum coverage requirement. In Alabama, for example, it's $10,000 (which isn't much for death or disfigurement). You will have this coverage in your policy unless you've waived it in writing. Don't do that. Insurance companies hate providing this coverage, and their agents often try to talk you out of it, and they never tell you that you can get more coverage for a very small, additional premium. Why insure yourself for less than you insure others? If you carry $100,000 liability coverage, increase your uninsured motorist coverage to that amount, too.

A related insurance feature is "stacking." Stacking allows you to combine the coverage of each vehicle you have insured with the insurance company. If you have two cars, each carrying $100,000 uninsured motorist coverage, you could make up to a $200,000 claim against your own carrier in the example of uninsured drunk driver. If you do make an uninsured motorist claim, your insurance company probably will drop your coverage. So what? You can get coverage elsewhere—a small price to pay for being able to make a substantial recovery that the deadbeat who hurt you cannot pay.

Here's another example of how good lawyers can make a recovery when all seems lost. You have a very good case with punitive damages. The defendant threatens to go bankrupt, but he's got a problem. The bankruptcy act doesn't allow a person to bankrupt a punitive damages judgment, nor does it allow someone to get out of other socially recognized obligations, such as alimony or child support. But suppose the defendant transfers his assets to his wife? No problem. If your lawyer can prove what the defendant has done, then the fraudulent transfer will be set aside by the court. This and the foregoing examples should convince you to go to a lawyer before buying the other side's hard luck story.

THE LUCK OF THE DRAW

Not long ago, a plaintiff's lawyer I know tried a major damage suit. His client was a paraplegic, a result of injuries received in an automobile accident. The theory of the case was based in product liability—a defective steering column that caused the plaintiff to lose control of the automobile and crash it. The case was tried before a jury and the defendant won. The plaintiff appealed and the case was reversed on a technicality. The case was then retried before a different jury. The same facts were presented, but the second jury returned a $2 million verdict for the plaintiff that was upheld on the second appeal. How can you predict outcomes like this? You can't.

SUMMATION

Okay, so now you believe the old saying, "A bird in the hand is worth two in the bush." There are hazards to any type litigation, whether you are a plaintiff or a defendant. That's why most good lawyers feel it's better to attempt to settle cases. There's another reason they feel this way, too, which is discussed in the next chapter.

12

Your Honor

THERE'S AN OLD BASEBALL JOKE that reminds me of judges. It goes like this.

Several umpires were sitting around a table in their favorite hangout, talking about how tough their jobs were. Their calls always made one side happy, the other mad. They were either booed by the fans or cursed by the players or their managers. Sometimes, they even had to throw unruly players or managers out of the game, which made them (the umpires) even more unpopular.

One of the umpires at the table was just sitting there, taking everything in and not saying much. Finally, a lull in the discussion occurred and he said:

"Well, here's how I see it. Some calls them balls, some calls them strikes, but they ain't nothing till I calls them!"

JUDGES ARE UMPIRES

There's very little difference between a trial judge and a baseball umpire, except perhaps their salaries, since both have the final say.

When lawyers argue about this or that point of law or whether or not something should be admitted into evidence, the judge, like an umpire, decides the issue. If lawyers or their clients get unruly, the judge orders them to behave. If they don't, the judge's bailiff removes them from the courtroom, out into the hall or perhaps over to the jail. At the end of the case, the judge tells the jury how to apply the law to the evidence in reaching a verdict, or, if there is no jury, then the judge decides who won or lost.

There are good, bad, and mediocre umpires. Judges are no different; some are simply better, wiser, and/or nicer than others, and some are horrible. It doesn't matter, though, because, as with umpires, what the judge says goes. That's all there is to it.

Because of their powers and ability to affect the outcome of your case, you need to know some things about how to deal with judges. If you are lucky, the one you end up with may like you and your case, and make you happy. This will save you the misfortune of losing or the trouble and expense of an appeal (discussed in the next chapter). Let's look at your first consideration about judges.

CHOOSING YOUR JUDGE

Judges differ greatly. One may tend to give harsh sentences to criminals, another easy sentences. One may tend to side with plaintiffs in damage suits, another with defendants. You certainly will want to get a judge who tends to rule favorably in your type of case. Unfortunately, this is often difficult, if not impossible, to do. Unless there is only one judge (then you have no choice at all), cases filed into the trial court will be assigned to the different judges on a first come/first serve basis. Once you are assigned to a judge, then you probably will have him for the rest of your case.

But, there may be ways to improve your chances of picking the judge you want, depending on how sharp your lawyer is. For instance, there was a time in my local divorce court when lawyers in the know would file a case and learn which judge the computer had selected. Then, if they didn't like the judge, they would dismiss the case and refile it. This process would be repeated until they got the judge they wanted. We had one judge who was very tough on spouses guilty of adultery. This judge, of course, ended up with more than his fair share of adultery cases, because the aggrieved spouse usually filed the divorce suit.

HOW THE JUDGE'S REPUTATION AFFECTS YOUR CASE

Once a judge is assigned to your case, your lawyer will have a better idea of how you might come out. For example, suppose you are charged with embezzlement (white-collar theft)—you "borrowed" $25,000 from your boss's payroll. The judge you draw is a "hanging" judge—doesn't like criminals at all, as evidenced by his harsh sentences. The threat of letting that judge try your case and influence the jury with his bias, or set your punishment if you are found guilty. should make you want to get the D.A. to settle.

Another example could be a good sex discrimination suit. The judge assigned to your case was a corporate lawyer before becoming a judge. He's never gotten over his animosity toward civil rights lawyers, who caused his corporate clients so much grief. The other side knows this and makes a lower than reasonable offer to settle. If you don't take it, you risk getting perhaps less, or even nothing. Then you will have to appeal to get things straightened out. Not much justice there, is there?

It works the other way, too. Take the divorce judge mentioned earlier who hated adultery. Your case is assigned to him and your spouse is wearing the big scarlet "A." The other side, fearing an adverse ruling, starts making settlement offers. Be patient, they will get better as you get closer to trial date. Settle during the trial, after the judge has heard enough about your spouse's misbehavior to draw a few scowling looks from him in your spouse's direction.

HOW JUDGES SETTLE CASES

In addition to knowing how the judge views your type of case, it's also important to know what role he likes to play in the settlement of cases. Many judges take a very active role in settlement "talk," as lawyers call it. Most judges are concerned with crowded dockets and long delays in getting trial dates, so they try to encourage settlement. Some do more than that: They force it, especially in the federal district (trial) courts.

For example, a plaintiff's lawyer had what he thought was a very good case, worth perhaps $300,000. The defendant's lawyer had offered $75,000 to settle the case. The judge asked them how far apart they were and was told the situation. "Well," he said to the plaintiff's lawyer, "this looks like a $125,000 case to me, and I think the defendant ought to offer you that and, if he does, you should take it." After a brief consultation with his client, the defendant's lawyer raised his offer to $125,000 and smiled. The plaintiff's lawyer courageously refused to settle. During the trial, the judge acted very similar to the judge in the movie *The Verdict* (see the Appendix). As in the movie, the jury returned a good verdict for the plaintiff, some $400,000. Then, on the defendant's motion, the judge cut the jury's verdict to $125,000 on the grounds that it was "excessive." The plaintiff's lawyer appealed the case and, nine months later, got the original verdict reinstated. The appellate court also awarded interest and a $40,000 affirmance fee (penalty).

Well, that case turned out okay—in the end. But suppose, instead, that the judge had suggested that the settlement figure should be $225,000. This would be closer to what the plaintiff's lawyer felt the case was worth. He might have taken it. Most judges who try to force settlements will suggest a figure that will tempt both sides. These judges are wise, unlike the vindictive judge in the above example, whose cases are often appealed and usually reversed.

Now, let's look at a criminal case I witnessed. Two defendants were each charged with four counts of auto theft. The judge told both defense lawyers that if their clients pleaded guilty, they would receive two-year sentences on each count, to be served concurrently (at the same time), meaning the total sentence would be two years. One defendant took the judge's offer; the other insisted on a trial. He was then convicted on all four counts and the judge gave him four two-year sentences to be served consecutively (one after another). In essence, the judge gave him an eight-year sentence, just for exercising his constitutional right to stand trial.

The examples given demonstrate two important points: first, that the judge in your case has the power to make it turn out much differently than the facts might justify; and, second, that if you reject the judge's settlement recommendation, he may overreact and hurt your case a lot more than you ever dreamed was possible.

JUDICIAL BEHAVIOR

As you have probably surmised by now, some judges are nice, polite, and try to do the right thing, whereas others are intolerable. Most fall somewhere in between. But regardless of how a judge acts toward you or your lawyer, it would be a good idea to say, "Yes, your Honor," "Thank you, your Honor."

The best way I know to make a judge behave is to have a court reporter at the trial. Court reporters take down all that is said and keep copies of all documents put into evidence or denied by the judge. In the old days, they used shorthand, but today, they either have phonetic transcribers that look like small typewriters, or they speak everything being said into a masked recording device.

Court reporters are your friends. Never, ever try an important case without one. Here's why. Judges typically behave better when a court reporter is being used. The judge knows that everything he says and does will be available for all of the world to read later on, including the appeals court, and if he's done something untoward, the judicial ethics commission may become involved.

Some judges will act nice in court, but, back in chambers, they will let their hair down and show their true bias. If your lawyer is experiencing this type of problem, he should insist on the court reporter being at those meetings as well. In fact, whenever anything important is happening in your case, the court reporter should be there. There are no exceptions to this rule, since, besides keeping your judge in line, the court reporter preserves the "record." The record is, in effect, everything that happened during the trial. Without a record, it's very difficult to appeal if you don't like the way the case turned out. Because a great many important things may happen in the judge's chambers, you will have an incomplete record unless the court reporter attends those private meetings.

Sometimes a judge will be so biased in a case that you may have no choice but to get rid of him. His bias can come out in several ways. For example, he can be openly rude to you and your lawyer in court for no apparent reason; his former partner represents the other side; before becoming a judge, he represented the other side's brother; he has publicly taken an antiabortion position and you are charged with illegal abortion; he is a member of the John Birch Society and you are charged with espionage; or he lets slip that he believes a woman's place is in the home, and you are suing your wife for a divorce because all she wants is to be a housewife.

If something like any of the examples happens in your case, your lawyer should file a motion asking the judge to "recuse" himself, which means disqualify himself from the case. Often when this is done, the judge becomes indignant, just like the lawyer who is guilty of malpractice but will not admit it. If the judge refuses to step down, then your lawyer will have the even more unenviable task of asking another judge or an appellate court to order that he do so. So much for your lawyer's future dealings with that judge, not to mention those of his unfortunate clients.

If it hasn't occurred to you yet, when you know what judge you have drawn, ask your lawyer how he and that judge get along. If you learn that the judge doesn't like him, get another lawyer on the case. You will be sorry if you don't. And it's a lot easier than getting a new judge.

CONTEMPT POWERS

Another thing that you should know about judges is that they have the power to enforce law and order in their courts. If you or your lawyer disobey an order of the judge, he will suggest that you reconsider your position—make you an offer that you can't refuse, so to speak. If you don't come around to the judge's way of thinking, he will hold you to be in contempt, meaning you will receive sanctions (a fine) and might spend the night in jail. The next morning, you will be brought before the judge to tell him if you have mended your ways. If you haven't, back to your cell with all of the hardened criminals. I can assure you that one night in a jail with thieves and rapists will have an amazing effect on your way of looking at things.

Judges use their contempt powers sparingly, but never think one who threatens to hold you in contempt is bluffing. Therefore, if the judge has ordered you to catch up on your child support payments or to turn over to the other side certain documents that damage your case, you'd better do it.

MAY WE APPROACH THE BENCH?

Now let's look at a courtroom procedure that confuses many people. Often in a case, especially a jury trial, one of the lawyers will ask if he and the other lawyer(s) may approach the bench. There follows a discussion you can't hear between the judge and the lawyers. Do not get paranoid when this happens. This is done to keep the jury, not you, from hearing what is being said.

For instance, your lawyer may fear that the other side is about to try to introduce some very prejudicial evidence against you, which he knows the judge will not allow. However, the other lawyer just wants the jury to hear the question—to get them thinking about it and wondering what you are trying to hide by objecting.

Suppose you are being sued as the result of an automobile accident. The other side has been seriously injured and you are at fault. The only real issue is the amount of the damages, and the plaintiff's lawyer wants the jury to know that you are wealthy and can pay a large judgment. So he starts to ask if you belong to the Running Brook Country Club. Sensing what's coming, your lawyer should call for a bench conference and get the judge to order the other lawyer not to ask the question.

On the other hand, lawyers often will approach the bench when they wish to introduce evidence that they feel may or may not be admissible. They fear that asking the question before the jury may be so prejudicial that, if the evidence is not admissible, the judge may have to declare a mistrial (dismiss the jurors and order that the case be retried at a later date). So, they approach the bench to ask for the judge's guidance.

For example, you are suing your partner for embezzling $50,000 from your business. He never reported the $50,000 as income and was caught by the IRS and convicted of income tax evasion. You want to introduce the conviction into your case to prove that it's already been decided that he took the money. Well, obviously, such evidence will win your case. The defendant will argue that it's too prejudicial— that it will take away his right to a fair trial. If your lawyer asks your partner about his conviction without the judge's permission, you might find to your dismay that the judge agrees with the defendant's objection. Then, the judge will order a mistrial, because your lawyer's question has poisoned the minds of the jurors. You will then have to get back in the long line of cases waiting for trial.

AFTER THE EVIDENCE IS IN

Another important (perhaps the most important) thing the judge does occurs at the end of the trial, after all of the evidence has been presented. In a jury trial, the judge will review the evidence and explain to the jury what laws apply to the case. For instance, suppose you are the plaintiff in an automobile accident case wherein the defendant drove his car into your lane and forced you off the road into a ditch. There is evidence that the defendant was going 55 in a 45-mile-per-hour zone. There is also evidence that the defendant lost control of his vehicle after it struck a large pothole in the road, which the defendant did not see because it was nighttime.

The judge would tell the jury that to drive 55 in a 45 zone is negligence as a matter of law. However, the judge would also tell the jury that it would have to find that the defendant's speeding was the actual cause of the accident. Then, it would be up to the jury to decide if, in fact, the defendant was driving over the speed limit and, if he was, that the speeding caused the accident. It could well be that the jury would find that the defendant's speeding had nothing to do with the accident—that the accident would have occurred had the defendant been driving at the lawful rate of speed. Thus, according to the judge's instruction, the jury would find for the defendant.

In a nonjury trial, the judge considers the law, then applies it to the facts. So, in the example given above, the judge would have made the decisions about whether the defendant was speeding and, if so, was that the cause of the accident.

Regardless of whether a judge or jury will decide your case, it should be clear by now that the judge will have a lot to say about how the case turns out.

SUMMATION

I clerked for a federal trial judge for fifteen months after graduating from law school. During that time, I was fortunate enough to see what goes on behind the scenes and learned the proper way to behave in front of a judge. (Sam Beatty, who often acted like a pompous judge in the classroom, was attempting in his own way to teach me this, too.) The judge for whom I worked was as fine a man as I've ever known. Even most of the criminals he sent to prison admired him. However, judges come in many flavors, and you should pay close attention to what your judge says, how he acts, and what your lawyer tells you about him.

Now, let's take a look at making an appeal, which is something that you may want to do if you lose your case. Unfortunately, it may also be something the other side will want to do if you win.

13

If You Lose the Case

WELL, AFTER WAITING three years to get your damage suit tried, you lost. Or, the jury didn't buy your alibi story, and it looks as if you are going away for awhile. In all likelihood, it's over and done with, even if you appeal, because only about 5 percent of appeals are successful. The other 95 percent are what is called "affirmed," meaning you have to live with how the trial ended. But even if you are lucky and win your appeal, you will still have quite a way to go, since an appeal is basically nothing more than a request for another trial.

WHAT HAPPENS ON APPEAL

The "appeals" court reviews the trial with 20-20 hindsight to determine if the trial judge made a mistake in the way he conducted the trial. No new evidence is presented at this level. The appeals court is looking for two things:

1. Do the facts reasonably support the result?
2. Did the trial judge misapply the law? If so, would applying the correct law have made any difference in the outcome?

In either case, the law requires that the trial court be given the benefit of the doubt. Take this following example on the issue of whether or not the facts support the result.

Suppose the case involved an automobile intersection crash. You were the plaintiff. You claimed to have the light going into the intersection; the defendant claimed he had it. The jury found for the defendant, even though you had more witnesses testify that you had the light than the defendant had saying you did not. Even if the appeals court feels that you have the better part of the evidence, it

106

will not disturb the result, because there was believable evidence to support the defendant's side of it.

Now, let's look at the second issue, the correct application of the law. Suppose at the trial of your case, the judge refused to allow you to present evidence that the defendant had caused three accidents in the past four years. The judge denied the evidence on the ground that it had no bearing on your case. This is the sort of ruling, on the law of evidence in this case, that the appeals court would examine.

Suppose that the appeals court decides that the trial judge was in error—that the defendant's driving record was so bad as to establish a pattern or a habit of bad driving. If that happens, then the case will be reversed and the trial court will be ordered by the appeals court to give you another trial.

Let's change the facts a little, though. Suppose that the defendant had two independent witnesses saying he, not you, had the light, and you had no witnesses except yourself. Your sole ground for the appeal is the trial court's adverse ruling on the defendant's prior driving record. Under those facts, the appeals court may say "So what?" to your legal argument—since even if the defendant's prior record had been allowed into evidence, the case would still have gone against you. The error was without injury. Here, you win the battle but lose the war.

WHO CAN APPEAL?

Either side can appeal a civil case. Take the automobile intersection example. Suppose you won but don't like the *amount* of the verdict. The defendant, on the other hand, doesn't like the verdict at all. You can appeal the amount, and the defendant can appeal the adverse outcome. In a criminal case, only the defendant can appeal an adverse jury verdict, because of the rule against double jeopardy—being tried twice for the same offense by the state or government.

APPEAL TACTICS

Defendants often appeal to stall the result. Suppose you are sentenced to five to ten years in prison for burglarizing a computer software store. You don't relish the thought of sleeping among murderers and rapists. So, you buy a little more time by filing an appeal.

Sometimes, with luck, you may buy more than a little more time. Suppose that while you're sweating it out, something wonderful happens for you. The appeals court rules in a case similar to yours that evidence against the defendant in that case was illegally obtained and could not be used against him. The same type of evidence was used against you. Your lawyer talks to the D.A. and your trial judge, and the conviction is set aside. By the time it comes up for trial again, the D.A.'s main witness has disappeared, so the charges against you are dropped.

Defendants who lose damage suits use the stalling tactic, too, hoping to hang on to their money a little longer. They also hope to get the appeals court to reduce the amount of your judgment, if not overturn it altogether. Take the biggest of all the Ford Pinto cases mentioned in Chapter 6. The jury verdict for the plaintiff was nearly $150 million, but the appeals court cut it to a meager $6 million.

On the other side of the coin, if a defendant loses a damage suit appeal, the appeals court will impose interest and an affirmance fee (penalty) in the plaintiff's favor. This is done to discourage defendants from using the appeals process to stall.

Enter now the trial judge into the drama. If he's like most judges, he doesn't like being reversed, so he does everything he can to discourage an appeal. For example, say you get a $2 million verdict on a serious personal injury case. Knowing the defendant probably will appeal, the trial judge may cut the verdict to $900,000 on the ground that the jury's verdict was "excessive." If the defendant appeals and loses, he faces having the $2 million verdict reinstated, plus interest and the affirmance fee. If you appeal, you may get a reversal and end up with nothing or having to try the case again. Crafty trial judges do this all the time.

Therefore, there is often a lot of settlement talk going on during an appeal. The negotiations and uncertainty never seem to end. Lawyers thrive on this way of living, financially and emotionally, but it's nerve-racking and costly to clients.

APPEALS SPECIALISTS

If you are taking an appeal, consider using an appeals specialist. Most trial firms will have one of these. If yours doesn't talk to the lawyer who tried your case about bringing an outsider in for the appeal. All of what was said in Chapters 7 and 8 about shopping for lawyers and negotiating their fees applies to locating an appeals specialist. And, be especially careful about the referral fee. Lawyers play that game here, too.

THE FEE

If you are the plaintiff in a damage suit and win, your lawyer will handle the defendant's appeal for you at no extra charge. He will still be working on a contingency—no-win, no-pay—basis. However, if you win the appeal, he will keep any affirmance fee (penalty) awarded against the defendant.

If, on the other hand, you lost the trial, your lawyer won't be as enthusiastic about taking an appeal. If he does agree to do it, though, the same no-win, no-pay arrangement should be used. If he won't work on that basis and if you still want to appeal, then you will have to pay him either by the hour or a flat fee (see Chapter 8) to do it.

As a losing defendant, regardless of the type of case, you will have to pay your lawyer to handle the appeal. He will not do it on an all-or-nothing basis. However, if you lost a criminal case and can't afford an appeals lawyer, then the government will provide one for you—usually a new lawyer with more time on his hands.

THE TRANSCRIPT

Besides the legal fee, you will have to pay for the transcript, which consists of the witnesses' testimony as taken down by the court reporter, all of the evidence, documents, and exhibits, the judge's instructions to the jury (or the judge's order in a nonjury case), and so forth. The transcript can cost several thousand dollars or more. If you were convicted of a crime, then the government will provide your transcript at no charge. Nice of them.

RES JUDICATA

Res judicata means "it's decided." Once your case is over, after all appeals have been taken or the time to take them has expired, the case cannot be filed again. You get only one bite at the apple. If you lost, it's just too bad. If you won, break out the champagne, unless you won a large damage suit and the defendant is bankrupt or doesn't have insurance. In that case, you really lost.

SUMMATION

The appeals process is something few people consider when they decide to get into a lawsuit—or when they are presented with one not of their choosing. But it's just more of the same give and take, though perhaps in a different form. As pointed out in the beginning of this chapter, appeals courts seldom reverse the trial court and order it to give you another trial. For that reason, you should carefully weigh any costs that you will incur by appealing against the slim chances that you will win.

This brings us to Part IV of my case. Up to know, we've been looking at lawyers and the legal system with the view of being able to improve the odds of your having a successful lawyer-client relationship. However, despite all efforts, the relationship may sour, or you may not be able to afford a lawyer, or even want to use one. If that is the case, then Part IV is for you.

PART IV

LEGAL MALPRACTICE, FREE LEGAL SERVICES, AND SELF-HELP

14

If Your Lawyer Messes Up

In this chapter, you will learn how to deal with unethical, dishonest, or incompetent lawyers. There are many ways to be hurt by a lawyer, and I hope that one doesn't hurt you. If he does, this chapter's purpose is to give you the tools and encouragement you will need to correct the problem.

Before getting into the remedies, let's outline the different types of problems that can be encountered.

TYPES OF LAWYER MISBEHAVIOR

Negligence or Ignorance. Your lawyer has done something unintentional that has injured your case, such as letting the statute of limitations run out before filing your lawsuit; failing to interview before trial the other side's witness, whose "unexpected" testimony destroys your case or sends you to prison; writing an ambiguous will that causes a client's heirs to litigate over what it means after the client dies; failing to notice a mechanic's lien against the home you are buying; or advising you that it's okay to shoot your neighbor's dog the next time it uses your yard.

Abusive or Unethical Acts. Your lawyer has done something that is gross, socially unacceptable, or violates his code of ethics. Examples of such misbehavior are seducing you while handling your divorce; pressuring you to settle a damage suit for less than it's worth so he can pay some bills; failing to tell you of an offer of settlement made by the other side; failing to advise you he has a conflict of interest and that you should seek another lawyer's advice; settling a case without your consent; using money held in trust for you to pay his bills; charging you for work never done; or taking your case and doing nothing on it.

General Incompetence. Your lawyer's life is such a wreck that he cannot effectively represent you, or he's just not sufficiently trained. For example, your lawyer is an alcoholic, drug addict, or compulsive gambler; is chronically ill; is fresh out of law school and doesn't know what he's doing; or talks a good game but is scared to death in court.

Once you realize that you are in one of those problem areas, you should try to do something about it—immediately. The quickest and usually necessary remedy is to get rid of your lawyer.

DISMISSING YOUR LAWYER

As a client, you can dismiss your lawyer whenever you wish. If he's done something in any of the three categories outlined above, then he's lost his claim to the lawyer's lien described in Chapter 4. However, before firing your lawyer, reread Chapter 10 on lawyer-killers to make sure you don't belong there. If you pass that test, then consider what follows.

Did He Really Do Something Wrong? Often clients get mad at their lawyer for reasons that have nothing to do with the quality of his work or unethical or abusive conduct. For instance, your lawyer has just told you that you should leave the makeup at home on the trial date, that he doesn't believe you are being truthful with him, or that your case isn't turning out right because your best witness is going to hurt the case. Or, he may have forgotten an appointment, doesn't return your telephone calls, doesn't keep you up to date, or doesn't get work done on time. Although in these instances his manners perhaps need improving, firing him may be a big mistake. He's already into your case and knows it better than anyone else. Bringing in a new lawyer may cause a significant delay. So, instead of shooting from the hip (and perhaps yourself in the foot), try this.

Seek Another Lawyer's Advice. Get a second opinion from another lawyer, but be warned. Many lawyers will not do this—the lawyer brotherhood problem again. If you can't find one who will, call your local bar association. *Calmly* explain what you want. *Do not* go into the details of your case. If you start ranting and raving, they will think you are a crackpot. *Never* tell them the name of your lawyer. The person you are talking to may be his best friend. If, after doing this, you still cannot locate a lawyer willing to give a second opinion, contact HALT (Americans for Legal Reform), Washington, D.C. They may be able to refer you to such a lawyer in your area.

Once you hire the second lawyer, let him look into your case and determine if your complaints about your lawyer are valid. If he tells you all is well, swallow your pride and stay with the first lawyer. If he agrees with your complaint, then start looking for a replacement.

When you seek a second opinion from a lawyer, let him know that he is not a potential replacement for the first lawyer. If you don't make it clear that the second lawyer is not a potential replacement, you run the risk of his thinking that if he tells you the first lawyer is doing okay, he (the second lawyer) is out of the case, or, if he tells you the first lawyer should be replaced, he (the second lawyer) gets the case. What is best for you might not be best for him. In other words, there is a conflict of interest if the second lawyer believes he might get the case.

If the second lawyer advises you to make a change, let him help you do it. By this I mean let him dismiss the first lawyer (or at least tell you how to do it) and hire his replacement. The reason for this is that both these acts can get very tricky, especially if your first lawyer has a big ego or is basically dishonest.

Hire the New Lawyer First. Before dismissing your present lawyer, line up the new one. This will save time, and the new lawyer should be able to help make the transition go smoothly. Hiring the replacement first also avoids the risk of being caught without a lawyer if you can't find another one willing to take the case.

Often, simply firing your lawyer can solve your problem with him. Sometimes, more must be done. If that is the case, then you can either file a grievance, sue for malpractice, or do both.

GRIEVANCES

Rest assured that no lawyer enjoys being investigated by a grievance committee of self-righteous lawyers—especially when he's guilty. Although grievance committees are made up of lawyers, they tend to deal with their wayward brothers rather severely—perhaps not as severely as you would like, but certainly more than the investigatee likes.

The Purpose of Grievances. Grievance proceedings are initiated and investigated when it appears that a lawyer has acted unethically or is incompetent. The types of lawyers described in paragraphs 3 through 5 at the beginning of this chapter are candidates for a grievance action. The purpose of a grievance proceeding is to punish the offender either by reprimand, suspension, or disbarment. Fines are sometimes imposed, too.

Righting the Wrong. Often a grievance proceeding (or the threat of one) can serve a second purpose. Take the example in Chapter 2 of my woodworking client whose deadbeat lawyer sat on the case. I advised my client to file a grievance against him. When she did, he decided to pay her the money owed by the defendant and then try to collect it himself. His earlier conduct had been very unethical, and he knew he could face a stiff penalty in the grievance proceeding— suspension from the practice of law or, perhaps, disbarment. As it turned out, the deadbeat received only a private reprimand. Although that punishment was too mild under the circumstances, my client did get her money as the result of the grievance.

This example demonstrates that the mere threat of a grievance can be very effective against a wayward lawyer in certain types of cases. However, if $180,000 instead of $1,800 had been involved, then threatening to or actually filing the grievance would not have recovered the money. The lawyer just wouldn't have had access to it. This isn't to say that a grievance should not be filed, only that to get the money, you would have to threaten or file a malpractice suit as well (which is discussed later).

Now, suppose that instead of sitting on the case for several months, the woodworking client's lawyer had taken on the case one week before the statute of limitations was to run out, but miscalculated and filed suit one day too late. This is an example of malpractice without abusive or unethical conduct. Better results would be had by threatening or filing a malpractice suit against the lawyer (as discussed below) than threatening or filing a grievance.

Prosecuting a Grievance. There's really very little to filing a grievance. Call your local bar association and ask how and where to file one. Again, be calm and do not disclose your lawyer's name. Also find out if there is a special form that is used and if the grievance must be notarized (sworn to). Then write down what your lawyer did wrong, either on the form or on stationery, have it notarized, if required, and send it to the proper place.

Before long you will be contacted by an investigator who will ask you questions and who will want the names, addresses, and telephone numbers of your witnesses, if any, and copies of any relevant documents. Unless the case is settled, you will be asked to testify at a hearing, as will any witnesses you have. So tell your witnesses about all of this and obtain written statements from them before you file the grievance, to make sure that they will testify for you. After the hearing, you will receive the grievance committee's decision.

If the case is serious, say, for example, your lawyer stole money due you, then you might consider hiring a second lawyer to prosecute the grievance. You probably will come out better using a lawyer in any event; however, you should weigh the extra cost against the additional satisfaction you will get out of pummeling your wicked lawyer a little more.

Filing a Grievance and a Malpractice Suit. In some cases, it will be appropriate to file both a grievance and a malpractice suit. Suppose that your lawyer stole $50,000 from you and can't pay it back. That is gross misbehavior and expensive to you. Naturally, you want both to punish him and get your money back. Take the case in Chapter 3 about the man who paid $200,000 too much for his business. The lawyer was guilty of a conflict of interest (a gross act), which cost the man a ton of money. In either of those cases, the lawyer should be punished *and* made to pay the damages. So you might file a grievance and hire a malpractice lawyer.

In such cases, the grievance proceeding may be put on hold when the malpractice suit is filed. The reason for that is if the lawyer is acquitted in the malpractice suit, then he will probably be innocent of ethical wrongdoing. But if he loses the malpractice suit, then he will almost certainly receive harsher punishment in the grievance proceeding. In either case, a wait-and-see approach is usually taken by the grievance committee.

However, if you intend to file a grievance against and sue your lawyer, hold off filing the grievance until you have received your malpractice attorney's permission to do so. He may not want the grievance proceeding cluttering up the lawsuit. For instance, I know of a case where a grievance and a malpractice suit were both filed. The lawyer's insurance carrier wanted to settle for a nice sum, but the lawyer would not do it because the settlement would not stop the grievance proceeding from being conducted by his state bar association. So, the case was tried and the lawyer won. The plaintiff got nothing. Had the grievance not been filed, the lawyer would have settled for a tidy sum to avoid the "hazards of litigation."

MALPRACTICE SUITS

In Chapter 4 I said that with the lawyer brotherhood it's difficult to get one lawyer to sue another—but it's not impossible.

Finding a Malpractice Lawyer. Most lawyers know which of their brethren will handle a malpractice case, and you should be able to find a good malpractice lawyer by any one of the following methods: ask a lawyer friend; hire a lawyer-broker to find one; call the president of your local bar association or the chairman of its grievance committee; or go down to the courthouse and ask the clerks or judges in the civil division. If you live in a small community, the lawyers there will know each other too well to handle your case. So, you probably will have to find an outsider to represent you. Your state bar association should be able to help you find your lawyer. Or, you can go to the nearest large city and locate one using the methods described above. If none of those methods work, contact HALT (Americans for Legal Reform), Washington D.C.

Meeting the Malpractice Lawyer. When you first meet with the malpractice lawyer, keep in mind that he is a rare breed. Therefore, you will not enjoy the choice of lawyers that you might otherwise have. A good deal of what I said earlier in this book about hiring a lawyer may not apply to this type of case. Here are some other things to keep in mind.

Suing lawyers doesn't win the malpractice lawyer any popularity awards with the brotherhood. For that reason, he probably will not want to take your case, unless it looks like an easy one to win and has a lot of damages. He will want to be well paid for being so unpopular.

That doesn't mean that you have to show him a million dollars in actual damages. In many instances, $50,000 (or even a lesser amount) can be plenty when the offending lawyer has been more than just negligent (careless). The reason is that lawyers owe their clients a very high duty of care, and any lawyer who misbehaves in exercising that duty stands to lose a lot more than just his client's out-of-pocket costs. The client can get those back, plus damages for mental anguish and suffering and punitive damages for the lawyer's misbehavior.

For example, if your lawyer stole $50,000 of your funds, you have a very good case for a malpractice lawyer. However, if your lawyer simply let the statute of limitations run out before filing a $50,000 lawsuit for you, then this is not nearly as good a case, because the recovery probably won't be more than $50,000. In the theft example, however, it could well be $1 million.

Malpractice Insurance. Most lawyers carry malpractice insurance. If yours doesn't, then your malpractice attorney may not be as interested in your case, especially if it's a potentially big one, because the defendant-to-be may not be able to pay the judgment or be in a position to discuss a large settlement to make you go away. A small case, on the other hand, may not pose this problem. Your ex-lawyer might scurry around to get that amount to stop the grievance and/or suit from being filed.

Malpractice Insurance Company Games. I have heard of some curious behavior of malpractice insurance carriers. For example, a lawyer-friend of mine inadvertently let a client's damage suit get dismissed. When he discovered what had happened, he tried to reinstate it—too late. So, he called his carrier and explained what had happened. The carrier's adjuster visited the lawyer's client, worked out a settlement, and then asked my friend to pay half of it (what his fee would have been). My friend's deductible was only $500, so he asked the adjuster why he had to pay more. The answer had nothing to do with his coverage.

"If you don't agree to this, he may sue you!" the adjuster said with a sly grin.

I guess he had enjoyed good success using this ploy on other lawyers. But I don't think he expected my friend's response.

"Well, if he does, he's going to get a lot more money than you have offered to pay, because I'm going to testify that he had a great case and I screwed it up royally."

My friend said that the look on the adjuster's face was memorable. My friend then paid $500 and the insurance company paid the rest. However, the adjuster's behavior reveals why the average lawyer is rather sensitive about his malpractice carrier. Most lawyers even will stall reporting a malpractice threat, fearing it will affect their rating with the carrier, and, thus, their insurance premium.

Another problem with malpractice carriers is that their adjusters often are unfamiliar with legal malpractice claims. In fact, they often are only automobile liability adjusters. That can cause some real problems—for the injured client as well as the offending lawyer.

The Suit. If you file the suit, the malpractice carrier's lawyers will defend it for your ex-lawyer. That means that your ex-lawyer, just like any other defendant represented by a defense lawyer, is likely to stall or drag out the case to wear you down—unless your case is a real nasty one. If so, you may get a good settlement offer early on. Lawyers aren't generally well liked these days and are what plaintiffs' lawyers call "target defendants," as are doctors, real estate agents, and large corporations.

Another frequent problem is lawyers with big egos, ones who find it impossible to admit they made a mistake. As a result, you may run into this situation: The malpractice carrier very much wants to settle, but the proud lawyer, determined to vindicate himself, refuses to settle at all. To him, settlement is tantamount to admitting wrongdoing. It's interesting to see lawyers who so often deal with self-righteous clients behave just as their stubborn clients do.

SUMMATION

I hope that you pick your lawyer carefully and that, as a result, you never have to fire him, file a grievance against him, or sue him. If you do, read this chapter again and get on with it. Your lawyer is a highly trained and well-paid professional. If he fouls up, he should pay the piper, just like anyone else.

15

Free Legal Services

I CONSIDERED not writing this chapter, because there's usually no free lunch—you get what you pay for. If you think that your lawyer-friend, who is handling your case as a favor, is working hard on it, then you're deluding yourself. He will push your case all around the top of his desk for weeks. Eventually, you will reliaze that you've made a mistake; perhaps you will even lose a friend. As a general rule, you should not try to get your lawyer to work for nothing. What follows are acceptable exceptions to this rule.

PREPAID LEGAL SERVICES PLANS

You may be able to obtain representation at no charge or at very reduced rates through a prepaid legal services plan. Such plans often are offered by employers to their employees or by labor unions to their members. There are also private plans available. To find out if a private plan is available in your area, contact *Public Citizen* magazine (founded by Ralph Nader) or HALT (Americans for Legal Reform), Washington, D.C.

Prepaid legal service plans provide legal services for the run-of-the-mill types of cases, such as divorces, small damage suits, wills, adoptions, buying and selling a home, simple bankruptcies or debtor's court, lease problems, and so forth. The lawyers who provide the legal services to plan members operate like legal clinics. Instead of paying as you go, though, you (or your employer or union) pay a fee resembling an insurance premium that enables you to get the law-yer's services when you need them.

LIABILITY INSURANCE

If you own a home or condominium, rent an apartment, drive a car, or operate a business, then you probably carry liability insurance. That type of insurance serves two functions: first, to pay claims others may make against you; and, second, to provide you with a defense lawyer.

Suppose, for instance, that you have a party and a guest steps on an ice cube on your kitchen floor, slips, and ruptures a disc; you chop down a tree onto your neighbor's house; your daughter crashes your car into a parked Mercedes-Benz; or while on an errand, your employee runs over a pedestrian. Those are liability insurance cases that your carrier will defend for nothing. Sounds great, huh? Remember, there's no free lunch. Take this scenario.

You have $50,000 coverage in the slipped disc case. Your "friend" sues you for $250,000 as a result of being permanently injured, unable to do the same kind of work and all of those other things that plaintiffs' lawyers dream about. The defense lawyer (or your carrier) feels the plaintiff is a malingerer and offers only $25,000 to settle the case. You want to offer $50,000 because your friend has told you on the side he only wants what you are insured for. (Don't tell your lawyer that you and the plaintiff had this discussion.) If the case goes to trial and the plaintiff gets a $125,000 judgment against you, then your carrier will still only have to pay $50,000, but now you get socked with the remaining $75,000.

Clearly, then, the defense lawyer has a conflict of interest between representing you and your carrier. He's never seen you before this case, but he handles several cases a month for your insurance company. Guess whom he will protect? What do you do?

Here's what to do to protect yourself. Write the lawyer a letter telling him you demand that your carrier offer to settle for the policy limits ($50,000 in this example). Otherwise, you will treat your carrier's failure to do so as negligence or bad faith and hold it responsible for any part of the judgment over the policy limits. Better still, hire a mean lawyer to do this for you.

As an aside, if you had been carrying an "umbrella" policy, then you would have had a lot more coverage. Most forms of liability insurance can be greatly increased at a very reasonable cost through umbrella coverage. Ask your insurance agent about this, before you have to defend a claim.

POOR PEOPLE

If you don't have a lot of money and cannot afford a lawyer's services, then you may be able to obtain free representation.

In criminal cases, you will be defended either by a court-appointed lawyer or the public defender. Public defender lawyers generally are more experienced than court-appointed lawyers, but it's usually an either-or deal. If there is a court-appointed system, then there won't be a public defender program, and vice versa.

In civil cases (other than plaintiffs' damage suits), you may qualify for representation through the federally funded Legal Services Corporation (formerly the Legal Aid Society). There may also be local versions of that organization, or perhaps the private lawyers in your area do *pro bono* (free) work for the poor. Call your local bar association to find out what's offered in your locality.

It has been my observation that the lawyers who participate in programs offering free legal services to the poor generally are very dedicated people. However, they are often overworked, fresh out of law school, or both. Regardless, they are lawyers, and you will be better off in most cases using one.

CLASS ACTIONS

Class actions are suits involving a lot of people, usually plaintiffs. Sometimes they are handled by private lawyers; at other times, they are handled by public interest law firms. In those cases, the plaintiffs all have basically the same gripe with the defendant. For example, an airliner crashes, killing 275 passengers; a company with South African diamond connections sells diamonds to thousands of unsuspecting investors for twice their true value; a real estate board conspires with its members to fix commissions at an artificially high level; a school system discriminates against black teachers; or a major corporation promotes men ahead of women with superior qualifications.

Those types of cases often end up in a class-action lawsuit. The court decides which law firm will control the plaintiffs' cases, and the court usually will decide the legal fees that the attorneys will receive. In cases such as the airline crash, the fee comes out of the recovery. In discrimination and price-fixing types of cases, the fee comes from the defendant—in addition to the recovery.

The courts tend to frown on class-action suits because they are very complex and take a long time to conclude. Also, in many cases, the chief beneficiaries are the lawyers, who may receive several million dollars in legal fees, while each individual plaintiff receives a nominal amount or something that is inappropriate in view of the damages actually suffered.

However, there is an argument in favor of class-action suits, and I believe it has great merit. If the lawyers weren't well rewarded, in many cases they wouldn't have gotten involved, and the defendant would have gone unpunished. An example of this is the "Agent Orange" case, brought on behalf of the many U.S. Vietnam veterans seriously injured by that substance. The case would never have been brought but for the potentially large attorney's fees.

REGULATORY AGENCIES

Often you can get the federal or your state government to handle your case for you. The types of cases that lend themselves to that process often also qualify as private class-action suits. In fact, those cases are sometimes prosecuted by private or public interest law firms side-by-side with regulatory agencies.

Examples of those types of cases, and the appropriate regulatory agencies, include the following: the diamond scam, real estate commission price-fixing, or Ford Pinto ready-to-explode cases—the Federal Trade Commission (FTC); the Tylenol tampering or Dalkon Shield/Rely tampon toxic shock case—the Federal Food and Drug Administration (FDA); real estate swindles or securities fraud—the Securities and Exchange Commission (SEC); the sex discrimination case—the Justice Department or American Civil Liberties Union (ACLU), a private regulatory agency, and so forth. There's also usually a state agency that corresponds to the federal agency, and it may be willing to get involved as well. To find out if you have a regulatory agency case, get in touch with *Public Citizen* magazine, HALT (Americans for Legal Reform), Washington, D.C., or your state's attorney general.

SUMMATION

But for the exceptions noted, it is better in most cases to pay your lawyer. In the first place, if you aren't paying for the work he does, you probably won't pay much attention to his suggestions. More important, if he's not getting paid, his heart may not be in your case. Look at it this way: Would you feel good about a doctor performing a serious operation on you without getting paid? Of course not.

That brings us to the end of working with a lawyer. The next and last chapter is for you do-it-yourself buffs.

16

Pro Se

IN LEGAL JARGON, when you represent yourself, you do it *pro se*, a Latin phrase meaning "for himself." There's another phrase that I used earlier: "He who has himself for a lawyer has a fool for a client."

Some of the worst legal problems I've ever seen were caused by lawyers, who are supposed to know what they are doing, trying to represent themselves. Even though they knew the law and legal procedures, they were too close to the case—couldn't be adviser-advocates to themselves. You will have the same problem plus one more—not knowing what you are doing.

ASK A LAWYER

It would probably be a good idea, if you are still planning to handle your own case, to consider buying an hour of a lawyer's time so that he can tell you how best to do it. For example, later in this chapter you will find some ideas about how to get around the dollar limit in small claims court. I've never read any self-help material that makes those suggestions. The lawyer you ask to help you plan your *pro se* case may have similar "clever" suggestions that will never occur to you. You should also request *pro se* literature from your local courts, consumer protection agency, or attorney general, as well as from *Public Citizen* magazine and HALT (Americans for Legal Reform), the last two located in Washington, D.C. Through those organizations, you should be able to get a pamphlet or book offering a step-by-step approach for what you want to do.

TYPES OF CASES

You will encounter one of three basic types of cases if you represent yourself. They are as follows:

126

Adversarial. You and another person are in a dispute that could end up in a lawsuit. For instance, you claim he owes you $500 and he denies the debt, or, you are charged with running a red light and have witnesses who will testify that the light changed to red only after you entered the intersection.

Nonadversarial Court Proceedings. You must go to court to get something done, but you aren't at war over it. Examples of this type of case are probating a will, recording a deed, adopting a child, changing your name, uncontested divorces, and so on.

Out-of-Court Matters. Falling into this category are writing your own will, drawing up a deed and getting it executed, drawing up a contract to buy a home or have one remodeled, and so forth.

Now that you know the nature of the different types of cases which you might encounter representing yourself, let's consider some of the risks of going *pro se*.

CAVEAT (WARNING)

In general, the more complex your case is, or the more money is involved in it, there is less of a likelihood that you will be able to handle it satisfactorily. For example, you are certainly entitled to handle your own six-figure damage suit or try your own divorce case. In fact, no court can stop you from doing so. However, not only will you aggravate everyone involved, including the judge and jury, you almost certainly will foul up the case.

Depending on where you live, nonadversarial court proceedings may or may not be open to you *pro se*. You will have to check the local court rules on this. But even where you can do it, the complex or large money nonadversarial cases are not something you should try to handle on your own.

As to the out-of-court category, there are no rules limiting what you can do—other than the rule of common sense. If you own only your house and a car, have a wife and no children, then perhaps you can safely write legal wills that leave everything to each other. Some people are better at this than others. But, if you make a mistake, you or your heirs may pay dearly for it later. Again, I suggest that you reread Chapter 5.

Okay, the lecture if over. The remainder of this chapter will outline some practical self-help remedies in the adversarial area, which is the area where you may be most tempted to resort to *pro se*.

SELF-HELP

You buy a used washing machine for $100, which carries a thirty-day warranty. A week later it quits running. The company from whom you bought it promised to send someone out right away, but no one came. They keep promising to come out every time you call, but you are now beginning to doubt their integrity. What can you do?

First, threaten to do something, such as file a small claims suit, get a lawyer, or call the Better Business Bureau or your local consumer protection agency. If that doesn't work, then try any, or all, of the following:

Better Business Bureau. If the used washing machine company is a member of the Better Business Bureau, file a complaint. The BBB will investigate, and perhaps put enough pressure on the ripoff artist to get your laundry clean again.

Consumer Protection Agency. You may have one of these in your city. If not, contact your state attorney general's office. File a complaint at the appropriate place nearest to you and hope that they can get results.

Small Claims Court. Last, but not least, sue in small claims court. Those courts are custom designed for small *pro se* lawsuits. In many areas, lawyers aren't even allowed in small claims—a do-it-your-selfer's paradise. I suggest this remedy last, because I prefer to avoid litigation. (However, be careful that you do not let the statute of limitations run out before you file the suit.)

SMALL CLAIMS COURT

To file a suit in small claims court, go to the courthouse with your checkbook and tell the clerk of the small claims court about your washing machine. Give him or her your name and address and those of the defendant and any witnesses and a check for the filing fee. The clerk will do the rest. You will be notified in due course of the trial date. If the case doesn't settle, be in court on that date with your witnesses and any documents that prove you bought a lemon and tell it to the judge. If you win, the judge will give the defendant a few days to pay, failing which the court will help you collect the amount of the judgment—if the defendant or his assets are still around.

There is a limit for which you can sue someone in small claims court, typically $500 to $1,000 dollars. If your claim is greater than that, you are required to waive the overage. But sometimes there are ways to increase the amount.

For example, a defendant drove his automobile into your parked truck, damaging it to the tune of $2,000. The small claims court limit is $1,000, but you and your wife own the truck jointly. Each of you can file a separate small claims court suit for $1,000 for the damage of your respective halves of the truck.

There also may be a court in your locality just above the small claims court, where suits up to, say, $5,000 can be brought. As in the small claims court, these cases are tried by a judge, not a jury. The procedure is almost identical to a small claims court suit, although the filing fee may be a little higher. If you have one of these courts, and, say, a $5,000 suit, file it there. Be prepared to face a lawyer at the trial though, and be prepared to lose if the other side does have a lawyer.

There's one curious thing about small claims courts: It may be illegal where you live for a corporation to file a lawsuit *pro se*. I never have understood this rule, but it's apparently widespread. So, if you are incorporated, you will be able to defend, but may not be able to start, a lawsuit *pro se*.

DE NOVO APPEALS

In most cases, either side may appeal a small claims court decision *de novo* (anew). The case is retried in a higher court (usually before a jury), as if it had never before been tried. For instance, if you lost your washing machine case in the small claims court, you could make an appeal *de novo* and get another trial. However, you would probably need a lawyer at that point, and the legal fees would make the cost of the appeal in this example prohibitive.

Besides small claims court decisions, *de novo* appeals are often allowed in certain other types of cases. Examples of such cases are nonjury criminal convictions in the city or county courts, rezoning and zoning variance decisions, condemnation decisions, will contest decisions, and insanity determinations.

De novo appeals should not be confused with the "review" appeals described in Chapter 13. However, as with review appeals, you will need a lawyer to make a *de novo* appeal, meaning that your efforts to avoid using a lawyer will have gone for naught. Therefore, you may wish to consider an alternative that avoids the courts altogether.

MEDIATION

More and more, I am hearing and reading about mediation services for people with legal disputes. Organizations that provide these services in your area may be the Better Business Bureau, the American Arbitration Association, or a Neighborhood Justice Center. Mediators help the parties try to resolve their differences but cannot impose a decision. And, if no agreement is reached, the parties can still fight it out in the courts.

Mediation services may be useful for common consumer complaints, such as automobile defects, as well as resolving marital disputes, neighborhood disagreements over boundary lines, automobile and homeowner insurance claims, and so forth.

Preparing for mediation is similar to preparing to try a lawsuit. The mediator will be acting somewhat like a judge, so be prepared to present your case in its most favorable light, which means that you should have any documents pertaining to the case in hand and any witnesses at the hearing (but only after a full dress rehearsal). It might not be a bad idea to allow a lawyer to help you prepare for the hearing. If the matter is complicated, you might even want the lawyer to go to the hearing with you.

When mediation successfully resolves a dispute, the parties are saved the large legal costs, long delays, and other hazards and aggravations of litigation. However, the results are usually in the form of a compromise, where neither side gets everything it wants. For that reason, and as a general guideline, mediation usually seems to work best when the money involved is not a large amount.

SPECIAL SITUATIONS

Sometimes there are alternatives to handling your own case or hiring a lawyer to do so. Again, this is where buying an hour of a lawyer's time might prove rewarding. The following are a couple of examples.

Suppose your ex-spouse stops making child support payments. You probably have a "family" court in your city (or county) that will help you collect what hasn't been paid and keep future payments coming in. This will be handled by government lawyers or employees at no cost to you.

What if you sell someone your second-hand car and the check he gives you bounces? Instead of going to small claims court, you probably can get better results by going to the district attorney and asking that a worthless check warrant be issued for the deadbeat's arrest. This sometimes gets quick results, since the judge will go a lot lighter on the defendant if he pays what he owes you.

A word of warning here. You cannot cause a worthless check

warrant to be issued just because someone gives you a bad check. The check has to pass to you at the same time or before you give up something in return for it. So, in the above example, if you had let your buying prospect drive the car for a few days before he gave you the check, you might not be able to get the warrant issued. Or, if the prospect had been renting the car, then decided to buy it and gave you the bad check, you definitely would not be able to get the warrant issued.

The different results caused by subtle changes in the facts of the last example demonstrate the hazards of going *pro se*. Another hazard is this: If you cause a warrant to be issued for someone's arrest and he is acquitted or the case is later dropped, then he can sue you for a lot of money. Then you will really be in a "distress zone."

SUMMATION

It's pretty obvious that I am cautious about handling legal problems *pro se*. About the only time you should travel through the legal arena *pro se* is when your case is not worth much more than what an honest, competent lawyer will charge you for handling it.

Closing Remarks

LADIES AND GENTLEMEN, I have done my level best to tell you how to hire and get the most out of your lawyer, at the least cost to you. I probably risked my neck with the brotherhood by writing this book. And perhaps some of the things I've said may have hurt your feelings as well. If not, then I've been a lousy adviser-advocate.

You may have noticed or wondered about the fact that this book does not discuss how specific cases are handled from beginning to end. This omission was intentional, for two reasons. First, there are many different types of cases, and it would have taken a 2,000-page book to describe all of them. More important, it's not necessary that you know at this point all that happens in a case. That's for your lawyer to tell you. Your job is to pick the best lawyer for you and your case, follow his advice, do your homework assignments, and not nag him—unless he needs it.

Before closing, let me again caution you about how you use this book. Do not browbeat or intimidate your lawyer with it. Use it instead as your friend and adviser—a silent partner so to speak—and whenever you're in doubt about what your lawyer is doing, refer to it. If that doesn't work, ask another lawyer what you should do.

Thank you for your careful and thoughtful consideration of what has been presented. I hope that it serves you well.

Appendix

MAKE-BELIEVE LAWYERS

MANY LAY PEOPLE with whom I talked while writing this book seemed more interested in discussing Hollywood productions about lawyers than real lawyers. So I have added this appendix to the book, hoping to correct any misunderstandings that may have been created by Hollywood producers, who sacrifice reality for profits. Let's look at some examples, beginning with the most famous Hollywood lawyer of all.

PERRY MASON

If you saw one episode of a Perry Mason courtroom drama, you saw them all. The ever-bumbling, overly sure district attorney, Hamilton Burger, criminally prosecutes Mason's clients in what initially appear to be airtight cases for the prosecution. Mason agrees to represent the apparent criminal without any qualms whatsoever. His fee, which one must assume to be quite healthy, is never discussed. Not to worry; his clients are usually people of means, to whom acquittal has no monetary limitation. Each case ends the same. Mason, having miraculously figured out who the real culprit is, leads him down the primrose path early in the trial, then cunningly closes the trap in a suspense-filled, dramatic series of questions, which force the culprit to admit guilt on the witness stand and acquit Mason's client, who lives happily ever after.

ANALYSIS

This may make for interesting viewing, but if you think that Perry Mason's cases remotely resemble a real case, you may find yourself in for a big surprise some day. For instance, you may really be guilty, a small detail Mason never had to face, and you might not have the money to pay the fee of a high caliber lawyer. So, rather than ending up with the fastest gun in town, you may instead find yourself being represented by some lesser lawyer, or perhaps even by an assistant public defender fresh out of law school.

One thing you can be sure of, your lawyer, unlike Perry Mason, may not believe you are innocent, but will act that way to keep you as a client and collect a fee. And you can be sure that there will be plenty of discussion about the fee and payment of the same before any work is done, especially in a criminal case. Why? Lawyers aren't dumb. If you stole from or murdered someone, what could possibly make the lawyer think that you won't cheat on the fee?

To be honest, though, I have watched and enjoyed many Perry Mason shows, and I'm sure that I will watch the reruns for years to come. His never-questioning loyalty to clients who appear to have no chance of acquittal should serve as a model to all lawyers, regardless of the type of cases they handle. Nevertheless, it is important to understand that Perry Mason is a fictitious lawyer, who represents fictitious clients, every one of whom is fictitiously rich and innocent. With that in mind, let's turn our attention to the traumatic area of domestic relations law and Dustin Hoffman.

KRAMER VS. KRAMER

This box-office bonanza came pretty close to real life. Hoffman, playing Ted Kramer, a rising advertising workaholic, comes home late in the evening after a busy day at work. His wife has just emotionally (and gutlessly) said, "Good-bye, I love you" to their five-year-old son, Billy, in his sleep. Now it's Ted's turn to learn that she is leaving them both. She is at her wits' end and just can't take it anymore.

A year and a half go by, and after a lot of tough going, Billy and his father establish a new life and a very deep love for each other. Billy hears from his mother (now divorced) on his birthday and at Christmas. Then Mrs. Kramer, having gotten her act together with professional help, returns to claim her son, who, of course, would rather stay with his father who hadn't run out on him.

Kramer hires Lawyer Shaughnessy for a whopping $15,000 to fight the custody suit. At the trial, Mrs. Kramer (who has also paid her lawyer handsomely) testifies that her problems were all caused by her former husband, who made her give up her career to become a mother and housewife. Now rehabilitated and having a higher-paying job than Mr. Kramer, she testifies that she should have custody of Billy because she is his mother, loves him, and should not be "penalized" for what Mr. Kramer caused. The trial ends with an emotional soliloquy in which Billy's father states that, as he understands it, the issue is not who wants the child, but what is best for the child.

Several days after the trial, Shaughnessy meets Kramer at a local saloon to give him the bad news—that the judge "bought the motherhood line all the way." Kramer vows to fight on, but loses his desire when he learns that to do so will involve putting Billy on the stand to testify that he doesn't wish to live with his mother. However, the movie ends happily when Mrs. Kramer has a change of heart. Understanding that taking Billy will hurt him as badly as her running out on him, she allows him to stay with his father.

ANALYSIS

First, let's look at the movie's good points. Of greatest significance is the graphic presentation of the trauma Billy suffers at the separation of his parents, which is compounded severalfold by the custody fight that follows. The contest is instituted by his mother's twin motivations—revenge against her oppressive ex-husband and satisfaction of her yet-to-be recognized (by her) guilt feelings. Seldom would a parent realize, as did Mr. Kramer, that the issue in a custody matter is the child's welfare, not the wishes or selfish needs of the parents. Mr. Kramer refused to put Billy to the task of choosing one parent over another. In real life, however, most parents would not be so unselfish, using the child instead as a weapon against the other parent—at the trial and for years thereafter.

Any lawyer or judge will tell you that a child custody case is the dirtiest, most upsetting type of case in which a person can become involved. For that reason, *Kramer vs. Kramer* is a very important movie. It is also important for bringing home the enormous financial and emotional costs of any bitter litigation.

Having said that, however, let's look at how the story was embellished to sell more tickets. In the first place, it is most unlikely that

Mrs. Kramer would have won the case in a real court. In a *change of custody* case, she would have had to prove two things: (1) that she was rehabilitated, and (2) that she could offer Billy a significantly better home than could his father. She proved rehabilitation but did not come close to proving the second point. Her wanting Billy or her feelings about being better for him, though impressive to a Hollywood judge, would have had no bearing on the second issue. However, the plot would not have worked very well if Mr. Kramer had won the case, so a basic rule of law was sacrificed to enrich the story—and the author and producer. Human nature was compromised, too, for if you think a real Mrs. Kramer would have voluntarily abandoned her costly and hard earned custody award, you would be sadly mistaken.

Disregarding the embellishments, *Kramer vs. Kramer* is a fair attempt to present a tough legal and moral issue. Now, let's take a look at Al Pacino in a no-holds-barred pounding of lawyers and the legal system.

. . . AND JUSTICE FOR ALL

The story begins in the city jail where Lawyer Kinkaid (Pacino) finds himself after having punched out one Judge Flemming, who had denied Kinkaid's motion for a new trial for an innocent client. The client, Jeff McCullough, wrongfully charged with a crime, had earlier agreed on the advice of an incompetent public defender to plead guilty just to get probation. The judge who had agreed to the plea bargain was off the day of the probation hearing, and the self-righteous Judge Flemming had heard the case instead. Flemming denied probation and gave McCullough a five-year sentence. Later, Kinkaid came to represent McCullough and marshaled enough evidence to justify a new trial. However, the evidence was introduced three days after a Hollywood-created statute of limitations for introducing such type of evidence had run, and Flemming denied the motion knowing full well that McCullough was probably innocent. So Kinkaid punched the judge.

Judge Flemming is subsequently charged with raping, sodomizing, and brutalizing a young woman. Since Kinkaid is known as a very ethical, nonpolitical lawyer and Flemming's archenemy, and since the case will certainly get extensive press coverage, Flemming seeks

Kinkaid out as his lawyer. Why? Kinkaid's accepting the case will deliver a message to the public to the effect that he thinks Flemming is innocent. Kinkaid commendably laughs in Flemming's face.

But another judge gives Kinkaid a word to the wise—that he agree to represent Judge Flemming or face disbarment. It seems that the legal ethics committee, headed by one of Flemming's bosom buddies, has discovered that Kinkaid once betrayed a client's confidence, causing him to go to the penitentiary. The client, a lunatic, was always telling Kinkaid of a fantasy in which he went around putting firecrackers in people's mouths. Much later, Kinkaid read in the newspaper that someone was going around holding people up with a pistol and making them put cherry bombs in their mouths. Remembering his old client's fantasy, Kinkaid tipped the police. Now, he finds himself being blackmailed with disbarment for having breached a client's confidence, unless he agrees to represent Flemming, the most despicable person he knows.

So Kinkaid reluctantly agrees to represent Flemming but tries to get him to do something about McCullough. Flemming, in turn, uses the McCullough case as bait, to keep Kinkaid working diligently on his (the judge's) case. Back in prison, McCullough, after experiencing multiple rape, sodomy, and beating, seizes a guard's revolver and hostages. Kinkaid goes to try to talk him into surrendering, only to witness his death at the hands of a police antiriot squad.

On the way back to his office, Kinkaid is accosted by an old client who gives him photographs of Flemming and the head of the ethics committee with whips, chains, boots, spurs, and naked women. Kinkaid now realizes for the first time that Flemming, who preached hell and damnation for all criminals and even those innocently accused, is guilty as charged. Wanting to resign from the case, he is dissuaded from doing so by his lawyer girlfriend, who reminds him, "It doesn't matter if he's guilty or not; your job as defense counsel is to defend him." Kinkaid then confronts Flemming, who admits guilt and even to having rigged a previously passed polygraph test and having manufactured a favorable eyewitness.

This brings us to the trial where the disillusioned Kinkaid tells the jury in his opening statement that "Winning is everything—not justice, not the truth"—that the words from the Pledge of Allegiance, "and justice for all" are meaningless in the legal system. Whereupon, he takes the law into his own hands, tells the jury that his client is guilty and renders justice that would otherwise have gone denied.

ANALYSIS

I think that it will be very difficult for me or anyone else to give a technical analysis of what is, in essence, a satirical romp through the "halls of justice." I don't doubt that most everything presented in the movie may or could have happened, somewhere, sometime, to somebody. But there's no way that it could all happen at once, and it's highly improbable that any of the travesties of the movie will ever be visited on you. However, it's clear that a valid public opinion statement—and a very unflattering one at that—has been made. In my opinion, all judges and lawyers should be required to see this movie.

Cutting through the satire, the story contains one serious flaw: the ending. No real lawyer would have convicted his own client, for such action would result in immediate disbarment—the very thing Kinkaid sought to avoid by agreeing to represent Judge Flemming.

In point of fact, Kinkaid did nothing wrong by reporting his cherry bomb client to the authorities. First, the lunatic was no longer a client. Second, lawyers are supposed to report impending crimes, even those which their own clients may commit. So, the threat of disbarment was merely a Hollywood contrivance that set up the dramatic, but impossible, ending.

Now let's look at a case where Paul Newman obtains both justice and *Ju$tice* for his client.

THE VERDICT

Unlike the satirical . . . *and Justice for All*, this blockbuster movie is nothing but a joke. It also is such a good example of Hollywood make-believe that it deserves a lot of space.

The story begins with Paul Newman playing Frank Galvin, an alcoholic, skid-row ambulance chaser, drinking beer for breakfast over a pinball machine in his favorite pub. He leaves there to check the obituaries, then on to the funeral parlors where he passes out his business card, pretending to have been an acquaintance of the deceased. Once a promising attorney, Galvin's career has been in constant decline following his having been forced to take the rap for an unsuccessful attempt by a senior partner to bribe a juror. Now Galvin has only one case left, a real honey of a malpractice suit against a Catholic hospital and its doctors, sent to him by a retired lawyer-friend and former associate, "Mick" Morrissey.

The case concerns a young mother, brain dead as a result of suffering cardiac arrest during the delivery of her last child, who died. Her husband abandoned her, taking their other children. She has been placed in a permanent-care facility by her sister and her husband, who are Galvin's "clients." Out of the huge damages they plan to collect, the sister and her husband will buy the victim a $50,000 endowment in a permanent-care facility and then use the rest for their own selfish needs.

The case hinges on the question of why a general anesthesia was given. The mother had just eaten before being admitted, and a general anesthesia should not have been given, because it would induce vomiting, choking, and, predictably, cardiac arrest. The admission chart states that the victim ate nine hours before admission, but her sister's testimony will be that she ate one hour before admission. The problem is in proving that the wrong anesthesia was given with knowledge of the facts about when the victim last ate.

A few days before the trial, Galvin goes to visit with the archbishop (the head of the hospital), who, in an effort to avoid publicity and apparently out of genuine concern for the victim, offers $210,000 in settlement. This is more than enough to buy the endowment, start a new life for the victim's sister, and pay Galvin $70,000 for having done virtually nothing. Seeing the case as an opportunity to redeem his career, Galvin self-righteously declines the offer, saying that justice will not be done, that he will be nothing more than an ambulance chaser—a distinction already achieved—if he accepts it. As you can imagine, his clients are hardly overjoyed to learn that he declined the offer without their knowledge.

Galvin next meets with Concannon, the defense lawyer, in the trial judge's office. The judge, a flaming Irish Catholic, is openly hostile to Galvin about the suit against his church's hospital and its physicians and does everything he can to get Galvin to take the offer. "If it were me, I would take it and run like a thief," he says, to which Galvin replies, tongue-in-cheek, "I'm sure you would." This thinly veiled barb, as you might imagine, does not set very well with the judge.

Then enters a beautiful young girl into the movie, a girl Galvin picks up in the pub. Unknown to him, or the audience, is the fact that she is really a lawyer for Concannon's firm, sent to infiltrate the plaintiff's side. And she does it beautifully, all the while passing critical information to Concannon. Unfortunately, she falls for Galvin, something she later comes to rue.

Galvin then goes to talk to his expert witness, only to find he's gone to the Caribbean for ten days—bought off, presumably, by Concannon. Hat in hand, Galvin goes to the judge's home seeking a continuance, which the judge gleefully denies. Next, Galvin calls Concannon at home to accept the offer—too late. Then begins a frantic search for another expert, which results in the landing of a seventy-odd-year-old, black general practitioner holding an honorary position on the staff of anesthesiology at a small hospital for women. This doctor tells Galvin that the attending doctors should have doubted the admission record information about when the victim last ate because she was complaining of indigestion in the delivery room.

The trial begins with Galvin's doctor on the stand. He testifies that the victim's brain damage was caused by her going some nine minutes without oxygen. The lack of oxygen was caused by her vomiting into her surgical mask, choking, and going into cardiac arrest. The judge then hostilely questions Galvin's expert as to whether or not the victim's going without oxygen for nine minutes in and of itself constituted negligence. The doctor, of course, has to reply, "no," to such a narrow question. Then the judge rules that the doctor has, in effect, testified that the hospital's doctors were not negligent and dismisses him from the stand before Galvin can ask any more questions.

The attending obstetrician is the next witness. He testifies that the delivery team did everything it could to save the mother and her child. On cross-examination, Galvin, instead of asking the doctor why he didn't doubt the admission record, for no apparent reason, asks him why it took nine minutes to get her heart working again. The doctor's unexpected reply: "Brain damage could have occurred in two minutes; she was anemic; less blood, less oxygen." Galvin has done a "no-no"—asking a question to which he, as Morrissey caustically points out, does not know the answer. The trial is adjourned for the weekend with things looking mighty bad for the home team.

Back at his office, Galvin and Morrissey pore over the medical records once again. Now it dawns on them, the attending obstetrics nurse, whom the defense is not calling to testify, must know something damaging to the defendants. Galvin goes to visit her, only to get the door slammed in his face. "You're all a bunch of whores," she screams at him. Smelling a rat, Galvin looks at the medical records again and realizes, incredibly for the first time, that another hospital employee, the *admission* nurse, Catlin Costello, who took down the victim's history, is not testifying either. The elated Galvin is yet again frustrated by the fact that Costello left the hospital's employ shortly after the incident and is not to be found. The mailman just happens to deliver the morning mail at this point, and in it just happens to be Galvin's monthly telephone bill. Galvin's face reveals the hatching of an idea, and he hurries to the obstetrics nurse's apartment, breaks open her mail box and pulls her telephone company bill, which also just happens to be there waiting on him. On it are several calls to the same number in New York City—to Catlin Costello, of course.

Galvin goes to New York, meets Costello, begs for help and then is met by Morrissey bearing shocking news. Back in Boston, Morrissey, while looking for a cigarette in the purse of Galvin's girlfriend, had found a large check payable to her from Concannon's firm. So Morrissey had dashed to New York to warn Galvin, who is on his way to meet his lady friend for a drink in a local bar. She has come to New York, too, ostensibly to take care of some matters involving her recent divorce. Galvin leaves Morrissey, meets his lady friend and punches her in the mouth, drawing blood. Then the action returns to Boston and the courtroom.

First, Galvin sets up the doctor defendant by getting him to admit that it would be criminal to give general anesthesia to someone who had just eaten. Then, to the defense's surprise (the mole having been symbolically silenced by the punch in the mouth), Galvin calls Costello as a rebuttal witness. She testifies that the victim told her that she had eaten just one hour before being admitted. Concannon then cross-examines her, falling into the same trap Galvin had—asking a question to which he also does not know the answer. "Were you lying when you wrote a 'nine,' or are you lying now?" To which she dramatically replies, "I didn't write a nine, I wrote a one!" She then pulls out a copy of the original admission record, showing a one instead of a nine. Then Concannon does it again, asking why she kept a copy. She says, "Because I thought that I might need it sometime." Not yet having learned his lesson, Concannon asks her why, and she blows him away, saying, "The doctor told me that he was tired that day and didn't even look at the admission record—that I should change the one to a nine, or I would never work as a nurse again."

You can imagine the look on Concannon's face about now. Not licked, though, he objects to the copy of the admission record because to admit it would presume alteration of the original—I'm not kidding—and the Hollywood judge, bushy eyebrow cocked at Galvin, agrees with the objection. Then Concannon objects to Costello's entire testimony on the grounds that, as a "surprise" rebuttal witness, her testimony can only be admitted with respect to the altered document, which was all she testified about; since the document was not admitted into evidence, neither can her testimony be admitted. The judge agrees with this objection, too, then tells the jury to disregard totally Costello's testimony and the copy of the admission record. The jury retires to deliberate, leaving a very dejected bunch in the plaintiff's corner.

In the next scene, the jury returns to announce, as everyone hopes, that they have found for the plaintiff, but wish to know if they can award more damages than the plaintiff has requested. The judge, bearing the look of the classic "trapped rat," has no choice but to tell them that there are no limits to what they can award. So the bad guys lose and *Ju$tice* prevails.

ANALYSIS

No sane lawyer would have referred this type of case to someone like Galvin. In the first place, he would be disbarred or sued by the client if Galvin fouled it up. Furthermore, any lawyer referring a case such as this would expect a tidy forwarding or "referral" fee out of Galvin's share of the recovery. Referring a case like this to a lawyer such as Galvin would, therefore, have been economic stupidity. And I really doubt that even a real deadbeat lawyer would risk disbarment for not passing an offer (of $210,000 in this case) on to the client. On the contrary, every lawyer I know would have leaned, if necessary, on his clients to take the offer and "run like a thief," as suggested by the judge. But then the movie would have ended before it started.

The utter lack of trial preparation, though plausible under the facts of the movie, would be highly implausible in real life. The deposition (out of court testimony) of the obstetrics nurse would have been taken by both sides and the "surprise" witness, Costello, flushed out early on. No decent defense law firm would have been surprised by Costello's testimony. If the obstetrics nurse had refused to testify on deposition about Costello, the lawyers could have asked the judge to order her to do so under penalty of contempt—the judge's order sounding something like, "Testify or bring your pajamas and toothbrush, because you are going to jail until you agree to testify!"

The use of a mole by Concannon, assuming it could happen, still rings false. He would not have used one of his own lawyers or paid her with a law firm check. The mole would have been an outsider, not traceable to the firm and would have been paid by anyone but an idiot in cash. Of course, without the check, Morrissey would never have discovered the mole's true role and the story would have ended a lot differently. In real life, however, getting caught doing something like this would mean immediate disbarment, which pretty much places the mole aspect of this case in the realm of a lawyer's wishful thinking. No doubt about it, any lawyer would love to have a spy working for the other side. But to actually do it? Only in Hollywood.

What about the judge? Few judges would have been so brazen as to deny Galvin's motion for a continuance when his expert witness, thus his entire case, disappeared on the eve of the trial. Such action would be reversible error (grounds for a new trial on appeal) and probably a breach of the Code of Judicial Ethics, which could have led to sanctions being levied against the judge—something judges, even crooked ones, usually try to avoid. The sustaining of Concannon's objections to Costello's testimony was also pure Hollywood invention. Take Costello's copy of the admission record. One of the more commonly accepted reasons for admitting a copy over the original in a trial is to prove that the original document has been altered. Yet, the judge disallowed the copy because it did just that. Furthermore, Costello testified to more than just the copy; she stated that the doctor ordered her to change the original, and that certainly would have been admissible, even if there had been no copy at all. Therefore, the judge's instruction to the jury that it totally disregard Costello's testimony was pure fantasy.

Be that as it may, after the judge got through with Galvin's case, there was no evidence of wrongdoing for the jurors to consider; they had been told to disregard Costello and Galvin's expert. Under such circumstances, the jury would have been told by a real judge that there was no evidence for them to consider, that he was ruling for the defendants and that they (the jurors) were excused. In other words, if all of this had really happened, there would not have been a "verdict." And the movie would not have been well attended either.

SUMMATION

The purpose of this Appendix was to bring those who saw and were influenced by those movies down to earth. By now, you should have a more realistic view of the modern Hollywood effect on the legal system. Hollywood producers must make money for their companies. Producing real cases—your type of case—usually doesn't create revenue for them. A couple of older movies, *Anatomy of a Murder* and *To Kill a Mockingbird*, offer something close to real life, if you're interested.

Glossary

This glossary translates into plain English a lot of the legal "mumbo jumbo" that lawyers use to keep you in the dark and thinking that the law is a great big mystery. If you can't locate the word you want here, I suggest you obtain a copy of any edition of *Black's Law Dictionary*. Most any lawyer or law library will have one.

ACCUSED.   One who is charged with committing a crime.

ACQUITTAL.   A finding of "not guilty" in a criminal case.

ACTION.   A lawsuit. *See* **CAUSE OF ACTION.**

AFFIDAVIT.   A written statement made under oath, usually before a notary public.

AGENT.   One who does something for another at their request.

ALLEGE.   To accuse someone of doing something.

ANSWER.   What a defendant says in writing in response to a plaintiff's allegations.

APPEAL.   To try to get the results of a lawsuit changed by a higher court. *See* **APPEALS COURT.**

APPEALS COURT.   The court that reviews the result reached in a lower court.

ATTORNEY.   Another name for a lawyer.

BAIL.   Money paid to stay out of jail pending being tried for a crime or after conviction while the case is on appeal.

BAILIFF.   The judge's bodyguard.

BARRISTER.   Another name for a lawyer.

BENCH.   Where the judge sits.

BREACH OF CONTRACT.   Agreeing to do something and not doing it.

BRIEF.   A written argument to the court about a case.

CASE.   What a lawyer calls the work he is doing for a client.

CAUSE OF ACTION.   The legal right to sue someone.

CIVIL CASE.   A noncriminal lawsuit.

COMMON LAW.   Law created by the courts.

COMPENSATORY DAMAGES.   What the wrong of another has cost the person injured (and not taxable as income). *See* **DAMAGES.**

COMPLAINT.   Lawsuit papers asking for damages or an injunction.

145

CONTEMPT. Being in violation of a court order. *See* **INJUNCTION.**

CONTRACT. Where two or more agree with each other to do something.

COUNSELOR AT LAW. Another name for a lawyer.

CREDITOR. Someone to whom you owe money.

CRIMINAL. One who has committed a crime.

DAMAGES. What a defendant owes a plaintiff for injuries the defendant has caused the plaintiff.

DAMAGE SUIT. A lawsuit asking for money damages. *See* **DAMAGES.**

DEBTOR. Someone who owes you money.

DEED. A bill of sale for real estate.

DEFAULT JUDGMENT. One side wins a lawsuit because the other side fails to show up.

DEFENDANT. In a civil action, the person or entity sued by the plaintiff; in a criminal case, the accused.

DEPOSITION. Out-of-court testimony of a party or witness to a lawsuit taken to see what they have to say or to be used in the place of their live testimony at trial.

DISCOVERY. The process of learning about the other side's case. *See* **DEPOSITION, INTERROGATORIES,** and **REQUEST FOR PRODUCTION.**

DISTRICT ATTORNEY. The state's or government's prosecuting attorney i.e., Hamilton Burger of television's "Perry Mason".

DIVERSITY CASE. Where the parties in a federal court are from different states.

DIVORCE. A court order dissolving a marriage.

DOUBLE JEOPARDY. Being tried twice for the same crime, which is prohibited by U.S. Constitution.

DUE PROCESS. The right to have your day in court.

EMBEZZLEMENT. Taking money or property entrusted to you by another.

EQUAL PROTECTION. The right to be treated by the law or government like everyone else.

EQUITY CASE. A case where the plaintiff asks the court to order the defendant to do or to stop doing something. *See* **INJUNCTION.**

EVICTION. A lawsuit to regain possession of real estate.

EVIDENCE. The testimony of witnesses, documents, and other physical objects introduced at trial to support the side of the party presenting it.

FEDERAL COURT. Where cases against the U.S. government or those involving U.S. laws or suits between citizens of different states are tried.

FEE. What the lawyer gets for his work.

FILE. The lawyer's record of a case. As a verb, to put something into court.

FRAUD. A lie used to cause another to do something (or not do something) to their damage. *See* **PUNITIVE DAMAGES.**

GARNISHMENT.   A court proceeding to collect money owed a debtor by a third party.

GRAND JURY.   Men and women asked by a district attorney to determine if there is sufficient evidence to prosecute someone for a crime.

GROUNDS.   Legal reason(s) for a suit or defense of one.

HABEAS CORPUS.   A legal action to bring someone or something before a court or judge.

HEIRS.   A dead person's surviving family. Sometimes called "next-of-kin."

INDICTMENT.   A finding of probable cause by a grand jury that a particular person has committed a crime and should be tried for it. *See* GRAND JURY.

INJUNCTION.   The court orders the defendant to either do or to stop doing something.

INTERROGATORIES.   Written questions asking what a party to a lawsuit knows about the case. *See* DISCOVERY.

INTESTATE.   Dying without a will. The opposite of TESTATE.

JUDGE.   The man or woman on the bench who tells everybody what to do.

JURISDICTION.   The right of a court to try a case. Not the same as VENUE.

JURY.   Men and women chosen by the lawyers in most civil and criminal cases to determine the outcome.

JURY INSTRUCTIONS.   What the judge tells the jury about how to decide the case.

JUSTICE.   What you are supposed to get in court.

LAW.   The common and statutory law. *See* COMMON LAW and STATUTES.

LAW CLERK.   The person, usually a law student or someone fresh out of law school, who looks up the law and runs errands for the judge.

LAWYER'S LIEN.   The right of an attorney to be paid for work done on a client's case.

LEGAL CLINIC.   A law firm that does simple legal cases efficiently and at reasonable fees.

LEGALESE.   Big words not in this Glossary that lawyers and judges use to make you think that practicing law is more mysterious or difficult than it really is. Often used by lawyers trying to gouge clients on the fee.

MALPRACTICE.   When a professional, such as a doctor or a lawyer, makes a mistake that injures his patient or client.

MISTRIAL.   When the judge stops a trial because a major error or gross mistake has been made.

MOTION.   A request that the court do something.

NEGLIGENCE.   A careless act that causes injury to person or property.

OBJECTION. One side to a lawsuit asks the judge to disallow evidence offered by the other side. Alternatively, one side disagrees with the judge's ruling on some point.

ORDER. A final decision by the judge.

PARTY. Anyone who is prosecuting or defending a lawsuit.

PLAINTIFF. The person or entity starting a lawsuit.

PLEADINGS. Lawsuit papers.

PROBATE. Pertaining to the estates of minors, incompetents, and dead people and real property records.

PRO SE. "For himself." Being your own lawyer.

PUNITIVE DAMAGES. Damages awarded against defendants who have acted despicably to punish them and to warn others like them that such behavior is not tolerated by society (and taxable as ordinary income).

REGULATION. An official interpretation of a statute.

REQUEST FOR PRODUCTION. A written request that a party to a lawsuit furnish documents or other physical evidence. *See* **DISCOVERY.**

RES JUDICATA. "It's been decided." The case cannot be brought again.

SOLICITOR. Another name for a lawyer.

STATUTE OF LIMITATIONS. The time limit for filing a civil lawsuit, prosecuting a person accused of committing a crime, or taking an appeal.

SUBPOENA. An order from the court requiring a person to testify either at trial or on deposition.

TESTATE. Dying with a will. The opposite of **INTESTATE.**

TORT. A wrongful act that causes injury to person or property.

TRUST. A complicated document most often used to preserve the assets of minor children, widows, or others not versed in business or able to manage money.

VENUE. The preferred place to bring a lawsuit. Not the same as **JURISDICTION.**

VERDICT. The jury's decision.

WILL. Also known as **LAST WILL AND TESTAMENT.** A written document, signed by the maker and witnessed by others, disposing of the maker's affairs after he or she dies.